RE

"War and Captivity. Life and Death. Fear and Bravery. A remarkable true story of World War II that takes us along through the hell of aerial combat against high odds, and the harsh life of survivors in Nazi prison camps. A tale well told, it gives us insight into the courage and character of our gallant young airmen who paved the way for the invasion of Fortress Europe and our ultimate victory over Hitler's Germany."

—*Major General Donald Ross, USAF (ret.)*

"Ray Parker's brilliant account of his extraordinary experiences in World War II, 'Down In Flames,' is -- without exaggeration -- breathtaking. He's got the spellbinder's gift. He catches the reader early on and never lets go. Intimate details of his journey from first awareness of the Great War to his near tragic involvement in it, his days as a prisoner of the Germans, all related with a visceral sense of detail, make for a wonderful read."

—*Lamont Johnson,*
Emmy Award-winning Director & Feature Film Producer

"Once I started reading 'Down in Flames,' I couldn't put it down. It's well written and kept me turning the pages. Ray Parker was head writer on my daily CBS-TV show, 'House Party,' but he never talked about bombing missions over Germany during World War II and surviving a Nazi prison camp. What a surprise! I can certainly recommend this book."

—*Art Linkletter*

"From planes spiraling down to earth in flames to the battling of wits with his Nazi captors, this inspiring memoir reveals the grim realities of the WWII air battle over the skies of Europe and the harsh life in a prisoner of war camp as can be told only by one who lived through it."

—*Bill Vega, retired VP of Research & Engineering,*
Convair Division of General Dynamics Corp.

"Ray Parker has written a wonderful and fascinating memoir of what it was like to be a young airman during WWII. Thrust into the chaos of war, shot down, captured, and surviving POW status, Ray's recollections remind us how extraordinary young men survived with grace, wit, humor and courage. A great read."

—*Colonel James R. Callard, USAF (ret)*

DOWN IN FLAMES

By RAY PARKER

Mill City Press, Inc.
212 3rd Avenue North, Suite 290
Minneapolis, MN 55401
612.455.2294
www.millcitypublishing.com

ISBN - 978-0-9640924-3-3
ISBN - 0-9640924-3-3
LCCN - 2008944162

Typeset by Peggy LeTrent

Printed in the United States of America

This book is dedicated to
all the gallant airmen
of the Mighty 8th Air Force
who gave their lives
to win the air war over Europe
that led to victory in World War II.

TABLE OF CONTENTS

ACKNOWLEDGMENTS

Writers often ask friends to read drafts of their work and make suggestions they feel might be helpful. I owe a special debt to Leonard Bird, Professor Emeritus of English at Ft. Lewis College, for his analysis of "Down In Flames" in its early stages that helped me shape the manuscript. He is the author of "Folding Paper Cranes," a moving memoir of Hiroshima after the U.S. dropped the atomic bomb to end World War II. Documentarian Christine Bonn searched for and helped select the photographs, and gave major editing assistance with the manuscript revisions. Her husband Mark created the book's cover as well as co-producing their recent documentary short about my wartime experiences that has won the Bonns several first place awards at film festivals. (See "In Times of War: Ray Parker's Story" at www.intimesofwar.us). Retired Air Force Col. Miguel Encinias, a fighter pilot and bunkmate of mine in a German POW camp, also contributed. Miguel, a hero's hero, went on to fly combat in the Korean and Viet Nam wars, and he served on President Clinton's Advisory Committee on the World War II Memorial in Washington, D.C. Col. James Callard, (Ret.) a Viet-Nam War helicopter pilot and former professor of national security policy and military strategy at the National War College (NWC) in Washington, D.C., was most helpful when I began writing this book. I'm also grateful for the counsel and friendship of J.William Vega, retired Vice President of Research Engineering of the Convair Division of General Dynamic, makers of the B-24 bomber in which I flew. Michael S. Simpson, the unit historian of my outfit, the 445th Heavy Bombardment Group, was always available to consult whenever needed. My memory over the decades got a boost from Mary Smith and Barbara Freer and their authoritative website, www.merkki.com. The website is all about Stalag Luft I, the German POW prison camp that by war's end housed nearly 9,000 of us Allied Airmen, including their dad, gunnery Sgt. Dick Williams, Jr. of Alabama. (Another great website is www.B24.net). Bob Chaput, a retired actuary and close friend shared his considerable computer expertise to guide the book manuscript to print. I am also grateful to insightful reader-friends such as Pat Hartman, Ingrid Ryan, Piper Moretti, Walter Dear, Richard Gibbs, Watson Lunt, and Lee Ray. Lastly, this book could not have been written without the endless patience and support of my wife Ethel, an ongoing inspiration in our life together for 44 wonderful years.

FOREWORD

"Of all the combat jobs in the American services during WWII, from infantryman to submariner, no job was more dangerous than that of a man in a bomber over Germany.

"The Eighth and Fifteenth Air Forces took a higher percentage of losses than any other American fighting force, from foxhole to destroyer deck. The air war was not clean or safe, it was murderous.

"Regardless of the continual banter between the bomber crews and the fighter pilots who flew escort for them, each held nothing but the highest respect for the other when it came down to doing their jobs. There was nothing more gut wrenching than watching a bomber go down and out of control with men trapped inside, or a fighter outnumbered and trying to fight off a swarm of German fighters to protect the bombers, then getting clobbered in the process. There were no foxholes in the air." [1]

Historian Roger A. Freeman praised the Mighty Eighth for its "remarkable esprit de corps, dogged bravery and supreme determination to succeed." Never once did a mission turn back because of enemy action – but the cost was high. Twenty-six thousand airmen were killed in action and 28,000 became Prisoners of War.

England's East Anglia region was like a giant aircraft carrier during the war, crammed with more than 130 air bases. These vast facilities could launch immense aerial armadas for 1000-plane raids that crippled the German war machine. Despite ferocious assaults by German fighters and massed anti-aircraft batteries of deadly accuracy, the Mighty Eighth targeted and destroyed German aircraft factories and U-boat installations, refineries, railways, power stations, naval bases and rocket launch sites. By war's end, 90% of Germany's infrastructure lay in ruins.

Dr. Kenneth Philip Werrell, Air Force historian, wrote that the Eighth dropped some 700,000 tons of bombs during its 33 months of action in WWII, losing nearly 6,000 heavy bombers. The bombers claimed destruction of more than 6,250 German fighters in the air, in addition to thousands of aircraft destroyed on airfields and in factories.

Along with the bombers, the Eighth's fighters claimed the destruction of more than 5,200 German fighters in the air and another 4,200 on the ground. The Eighth fought the air war over Western Europe along with British Bomber Command, other American strategic bombers based in Italy, and the Allied tactical air forces.

Dr. Werrell quoted the postwar United States Strategic Bombing Survey as saying:

"Allied air power was decisive in the war in Western Europe. Hindsight inevitably suggests that it might have been employed differently or better in some respects. Nevertheless, it was decisive. In the air, its victory was complete; at sea, its contribution, combined with naval power, brought an end to the enemy's greatest naval threat—the U-boat; on land, it helped turn the tide overwhelmingly in favor of Allied ground forces. Its power and superiority made possible the success of the invasion. It brought the economy which sustained the enemy's armed forces to virtual collapse, although the full effects of this collapse had not reached the enemy's front lines when they were overrun by Allied forces."

The Eighth's primary accomplishment, Dr. Werrell said, was "the defeat of Germany's air force. At the same time it weakened both her industry and her war effort."[2] Destruction of the German Luftwaffe gave the Allies complete air superiority over the Normandy beaches when the invasion of Europe came on June 6, 1944.

What did the Germans have to say about our massive strategic bombing campaign?[3]

Albert Speer, Hitler's Minister for Armaments and Economics:

"The strategic bombing of Germany was the greatest lost battle of the World War for Germany."

General Adolph Galland, commander of the Luftwaffe's fighter group:

"The bombers grounded our fighters by destroying our oil industry."

Field Marshall Erwin Rommel, speaking to the German High Command in June '44:

"If you cannot stop the bombing we cannot win."

German Army General Sepp Dietrich, when ordered by Hitler to continue his advance during the Battle of the Bulge, responded:

"'Go on? Go on? How can we go on? We have no ammunition left and all our supply lines have been cut by air attack. People don't understand that not even the best troops can stand this mass bombing. One experience of it and they lose all their fighting spirit."

Luftwaffe Field Marshall Hugo Sperrie:

"Allied Air power was the chief factor in Germany's defeat."

CHAPTER ONE

A DAY OF INFAMY

ights are burning in the pre-dawn darkness on the second floor of the ornate old Los Angeles Examiner building. The final morning edition has already gone to bed. Only two of us staffers are on duty in the editorial room on this quiet Sunday morning. Sitting at the massive wooden city desk, wearing his green eyeshade is the night city editor, Baker Conrad, a soft-spoken news veteran in his fifties. He's smart and experienced enough to rate a key day assignment on this major metropolitan daily, but he prefers the solitude of the night. I am his copy boy for the graveyard shift, the humblest job on the paper. The calm and ordinarily unflappable Mr. Conrad is idly leafing through the pages of the rival Los Angeles Times, waiting for something newsworthy to happen. I am sitting across from him, half-dozing while trying to study a fat chemistry textbook for a major exam at City College. I had peddled the Sunday Examiner from a toy red wagon as a grammar school kid in the depths of the Great Depression. Now I'm actually working here, dreaming of being a real newspaperman myself some day with a byline on the front page.

Suddenly all the news service Teletype machines start hammering out news bulletins with a chorus of bells clamoring for attention. Something big is happening! I run to the machines, ripping off bulletins. I read the first few paragraphs in shock and disbelief, then hurry back to thrust them into the editor's hands.

"The Japanese have bombed Pearl Harbor!" I tell him.

His hands are trembling as he reads on. "Oh, my God," he says. "We're at war!"

"Umm, where's Pearl Harbor?" I ask. I didn't know, but like many millions of other Americans, I'd remember this day—December 7, 1941 – for the rest of my life.

"It's a huge naval base in Hawaii for our entire Pacific Fleet," he answered. "Christ! The Japs caught our ships by surprise, like sitting ducks!"

Mr. Conrad snatches up his phone to rouse the managing editor from bed with the dreadful news. The teletypes are still clattering away with more disastrous details of warships on fire and sinking after a devastating sneak attack by squadrons of Japanese carrier-based bombers and fighter planes. Within minutes, more than a thousand young American Navy men aboard our battlewagons, cruisers and destroyers caught at anchor lose their lives.

The USS *Arizona* explodes, hit by a 1,760-pound armor-piercing shell that slams through her deck and ignites her forward ammunition magazine. She sinks in nine minutes with 1,177 of her crew entombed forever. The USS *Oklahoma*, hit by several torpedoes, rolls over, trapping more than 400 men inside. The USS *California* and USS *West Virginia* sink at their moorings. The USS *Utah* capsizes with more than 50 of her crew. The USS *Maryland*, USS *Pennsylvania*, and USS *Tennessee* and the USS *Shaw* all suffer serious damage. The USS *Nevada* attempts to run out to sea but takes several crippling hits and has to be run aground to avoid sinking and blocking the harbor entrance.

As the grim news keeps flooding in, it becomes obvious that this is the worst military disaster in our history. In the words of President Franklin Delano Roosevelt, it is "A day that will live in infamy." Soon the Examiner's editors and reporters will be streaming in to assemble a special wartime edition for more than half a million readers. The Examiner, the flagship of the Hearst newspaper chain, is the biggest and most readable paper in town.

I hang around when my shift ends, hoping to get some fatherly advice from Mr. Conrad. My father took my mom and kid brother back to live in our native Ohio a year ago after I graduated here from high school. The Great Depression isn't over yet, and dad was hoping he could get a better job by moving back to Cleveland where his old business buddies live. I chose to stay behind so I could get a college education as a legal resident

Direct hit on the USS Shaw at Pearl Harbor.

"A Day of Infamy!"

of California. I'm now rooming at a modest boarding house run by Mrs. Zimmerman, a proper widow with graying black hair done up in a bun. All her roomers are young working people, with me as the youngest.

As the graveyard shift ends at dawn, Mr. Conrad pushes away from his desk and grabs his hat and coat. I have tremendous respect for this man, so I'm anxious to hear what he might say about a plan that I can't stop thinking about.

"Mr. Conrad, do you have a moment?"

He nods agreeably. "Sure. What's on your mind, Ray?"

"I've been thinking for some time about joining the Army Air Corps. Now that we're at war, I want to volunteer for pilot training."

I thought he'd be proud of me, but instead he just stares and asks, "How old are you?

"Eighteen, sir."

He frowns. "What's the rush? When Uncle Sam wants you, believe me, he'll call you."

"I know, sir, but the Army Air Corps is enlisting young guys like me right now to become flyers. If I don't sign up soon, I might miss my chance."

He gestures to my stack of textbooks. "What about college? If you want to be a newspaperman, you'll need to finish college to have a decent career in this business."

"Yes sir, but I figure I can do that when the war's over. They need pilots now."

"What about your folks? What do they say?"

I have to confess I haven't talked it over with mom and dad yet.

He shakes his head. "Well, for what it's worth, I think you should stay in school and get a college deferment. We're probably in for another long and frightful war like the last one—or even worse! You'll have plenty of chances to serve your country when the time comes."

With that he smiles, pats me on the shoulder and heads for the door. I just stand there, remembering how kind and encouraging he's been since the day I came to work for him six months ago. Although I'm only a copyboy, he's been helping me gain practical experience by letting me write lots of small stories and obits. He's even told me I have a future as a newspaperman. Yet here I am, disappointing him. Not only have I made up my mind, I can't wait to enlist.

A Chance to Volunteer

I call mom and dad tonight about my intention to volunteer. Not surprisingly, they feel the same as Mr. Conrad, but I insist it's my decision to make. Besides, as dad has to admit, everyone my age will be in uniform sooner or later anyhow. He had tried to enlist in World War I, but the medics wouldn't take him because he'd suffered a throat injury from a hard-thrown baseball in a bush league game in Cleveland. He was waving to his girl friend in the grandstands—my mom to be—and didn't see the ball coming.

I'd been trying to decide lately whether to join the Royal Canadian Air Force or wait until the USA joined the conflict. The RCAF has an office in the Hollywood Roosevelt Hotel where they recruit young Americans. Elements of the RCAF are already shooting down Nazi warplanes over England in the Battle of Britain, flying side by side with my personal heroes, the fighter pilots of the Royal Air Force.

Every evening I turn on my old Philco radio to hear CBS war correspondent Edward R. Murrow say, "This is London calling." He then gives us listeners vivid word pictures of Nazi bombs raining down in the heart of the city, and aerial dogfights in the skies. Ever since the British Army was driven back onto the beaches of Dunkirk by the Nazi war machine in an overwhelming defeat, the RAF has been all that stands between the British people and a German invasion.

Now, with America at war, I decide to cut my Monday morning chemistry class and take a streetcar downtown to the Army Air Corps recruiting office. It's already jammed with excited volunteers lining up for interviews. When I finally reach a recruiting sergeant's desk, he takes a skeptical look at my skinny frame and asks my age. I tell him.

"Any college yet?"

"Just started this semester, sir."

"The Army Air Corps is looking for volunteers who've had at least two years of college."

"I know, but I read that they're waiving that requirement for anyone who can pass a two-year college equivalent exam."

He sits back and smiles. "True. But that exam is pretty tough."

"I'd still like to take it, sir."

"Well, you can." It isn't his job to turn volunteers away. He takes down my name, address and telephone number. "The next examination will be Friday morning at ten o'clock. Can you make it?"

"Yes sir!"

Handing over a mimeographed sheet, he says, "Here's where you report. "

"Thank you, sir!"

He grins. "And you don't say 'sir' to non-commissioned officers like me."

"No sir!"

This time he laughs.

I think of little else for the next several days until it's time to show up for the exam at a bungalow classroom near downtown. A testing supervisor greets about 40 of us aviation cadet wannabes as we come in and take seats at desks.

"This is a timed test, exactly one hour long," the supervisor says. As soon as monitors hand out pencils and exam papers, he gestures with a stopwatch and says, "Begin now."

I skim through all the questions first, answering those I know for certain and skipping those that will take more time. Then I double back and answer the rest, occasionally taking a guess at the most logical answer.

As I hand in the exam, the instructor whispers, "There's still more time if you need it."

I shake my head. For better or worse, I've done my best. The test was difficult, as the sergeant had predicted, but not as brain racking as I feared. I leave feeling fairly optimistic.

A Mysterious Caller

That night at Mrs. Zimmerman's boarding house, as the roast chicken and mashed potatoes are passed around, everyone is talking at once about the war. President Roosevelt has just been on the radio, denouncing the Japanese sneak attack. The news from Pearl Harbor is getting even worse as more details of mounting casualties and destruction keep coming in. There are even rumors that the Japanese might soon be attacking California.

The next morning at breakfast Mrs. Zimmerman comes in and says I have a call on the hallway phone from the Army Air Corps. "Mr. Parker," says a man's voice, "we want you to come in this morning to discuss the results of your cadet qualification test."

"Yes sir, I will. Can you tell me how I did?"

"You did well, but we need to talk."

I have no idea what the caller means, nor does he tell me. When I show up for the meeting, I'm surprised to see it's with an Army Air Corps Major. My exam is lying on his desk. He wastes no time coming to the point.

"Mr. Parker, I'm sorry this conversation is necessary. We have reason to suspect that you already knew the answers on our test, and if so, we must know how that happened."

What? He's accusing me of cheating? I have to protest, "I didn't cheat, sir. May I ask what makes you think I did?"

He holds up his hand for silence. "I'll ask the questions. The Army Air Force must be very careful in selecting candidates because cadets become commissioned officers when they graduate from training. I'm sure you understand that we cannot make officers out of liars and cheats."

His blunt language stings. "Yes, of course sir." Even though I've done nothing wrong, I could still be in real trouble. How can I convince him I didn't know the answers in advance?

He gives me a long, piercing look. I'm getting nervous, my heart is pounding and I'm feeling very uncomfortable.

"Mr. Parker, this is an extremely serious matter. If our security has been compromised and you can tell us how, it will go much easier for you."

"But, sir!" I protest, "I didn't cheat."

He waves my exam papers in my face. "You're telling me that you never saw those questions before the test?"

"That's right, sir."

His eyes are drilling right through me.

"Mr. Parker, you are 18 years old, and in your freshman year at Los Angeles City College. Is that correct?"

"Yes sir."

"Yet you managed to score third highest in Los Angeles on this very comprehensive examination."

"Third highest?" So that's it! No wonder they suspect something.

"We want to know how you accomplished this."

Good question. I thought I'd done well, but not that well. What can I say? All I can do is tell him the truth and hope for the best.

"I've done a lot of reading since I was six years old, so I probably have a bigger vocabulary and know more facts about the world than most young people my age. I read several books a week in grammar school."

The Major nods non-committally, so I keep going. "I've also taken a lot of exams for college prep courses, so you might say I'm kind of test-wise."

"What do you mean, 'test-wise'?"

"I've learned to leave the tougher questions for last on any timed test to make sure I answer all the ones I know first. Then I use whatever time remains to work on the longer ones, and make guesses on the rest."

That was it. There's really nothing else I can say.

The Major sits quietly for a while, absently tapping his pencil on my exam and gazing off into space. Finally he pushes the exam aside, smiles for the first time and says "I used to take tests that way myself. Makes sense to me."

Woooh! What a relief it is to hear those words.

Now he's all business again. "You'll be sworn in as a cadet and go on furlough for 90 days until we have room for you to begin training at Santa Ana Army Air Base. What do you prefer to be? Pilot, navigator or bombardier? You've qualified for all three."

That was easy. "A pilot, sir."

"Very well." He makes a note and stands up to reach over the desk and shake my hand. "Glad to have you with us."

I give him a rather clammy hand because he really shook me up, but I've seldom been happier in my entire life than I am at this moment.

Looking back now after all the decades since World War II, and knowing how narrowly I escaped death in combat, I marvel at how easily young men can decide to volunteer as I did to put their lives on the line for their country. It happens generation after generation. Why? How do volunteers differ from others who wait for the draft and those who hope they won't have to go at all? One basic difference in my case must have been how naive I was about war. I gave little thought to the possibility of coming home in a flag-draped casket or a wheelchair. That might happen to the other guy, but not me. I was also idealistic, as young people usually are. I felt a great love of country, inspired by the words and deeds of President Franklin Delano Roosevelt. His vision and wisdom helped transform the United States from a totally unprepared land of isolationists to a mighty nation that did indeed save the world for democracy. FDR personified every decent and precious thing I still admire most about the United States of America.

CHAPTER TWO

THE FLEDGLINGS

If you were destined to be a flying officer, the Army Air Corps first sent you to Southern California for pre-flight training at a boot camp for aviation cadets known as Santa Ana Army Air Base. It was an immense installation, sprawling across nearly 1,700,000 acres that today embrace the city of Costa Mesa and two college campuses, as well as other schools, fairgrounds and commercial, industrial and residential areas. Future pilots, navigators and bombardiers came here to learn the basics of military life and take intensive classes in aviation-related skills such as meteorology, Morse code and identifying the silhouettes of enemy fighter planes and warships.

But when I arrive at camp on an Army bus with dozens of other volunteers in the spring of 1942, the base has been open less than two months. Barracks buildings are popping up everywhere in a giant housing project that is running on fast-forward. Even so, there are no barracks ready for our busload yet. Just tents.

I duck inside my assigned tent and find a cadet already settling in. He's a wiry redhead about my size, stretched out on a bunk in his brand new olive drab uniform. He's Mike Boomer, a witty and mischievous character from Detroit who'll soon become my best buddy. A year or so older than I, Mike joined the regular Army during the Great Depression of the Thirties. In those hardscrabble days, a job was a job and you were damned glad to have one. But the moment the USA entered World War II, Mike applied for cadet training in the Army Air Corps.

Mike offers to show me around. "Let's go see the telephone building where there are lots of booths for making calls," he says. "It's easy. Just go in a booth and tell the operator your name and the number to dial. When the call goes through, she pages you and sends you to a booth to take it." So, off we go to a building nearby where a staff of female operators somewhere upstairs are placing calls for a dozen or so cadets. As Mike ducks into a phone booth, I hear voices over a loudspeaker, directing cadets where to go. Soon I hear a young woman's voice calling out a first and last name which, when said together, create a "name" too bawdy to repeat in print. She says it several times while cadets all over the office burst into laughter. Suddenly we hear an embarrassed gulp on the loudspeaker—and then silence. Mike comes out of his phone booth, practically falling down laughing, with that mischievous grin on his face betraying that he's the culprit.

He and I spend most of our free time—what there is of it!—together. Wise in Army ways, he helps me avoid trouble with our cadet officer superiors that results in punishments including running laps around the track or KP (kitchen police) duty at the mess hall.

Getting Needled

The first days at Santa Ana feel like a dizzying ride on a mass production belt. There are lines for physical checkups, lines for blood tests—it seems endless. Medics extract blood with huge needles so intimidating that some cadets keel over in a faint. All fainters are rejected for flight training. It's not much fun either to be immunized against everything from diphtheria to lockjaw. God help you if you ever lose your personal shot records, because the medics will ignore your protests and jab you all over again. I go through a medical gauntlet with needlers on each side who give shots in stereo. While I am frantically waving my shot record at the needler on my left, his buddy skewers me with a shot I've already had. Worse yet, I find out the hard way that one of those needles wasn't sterile. I spend the next two days lying on my sleeping cot, utterly miserable, jaundiced and turning yellow as a lemon.

Endless Parades

After we survive all the medical work, the Army Air Corps sets about training us as soldiers. You might not think that aviation cadets would need to learn to march like the infantry and learn the manual of arms—a fancy bit of rifle twirling and tossing that looks great on parade grounds—but we do. We also are drilled, hour after hour, to learn how to march in close formation.

Every Sunday we have to show our stuff, passing in review for the camp senior officers and their ladies sitting in the bleachers, relaxed and comfy with their hats and parasols as we come sweating by under a blazing summer sun in swirling clouds of dust.

That formal Sunday parade in dress uniform is every cadet's favorite groaner. We march in separate units, pilots-to-be with pilots, navigators with navigators and bombardiers with bombardiers.

From the reviewing stand it must have been easy to spot the approaching navigator formations, because they didn't so much march as slouch along out of step. The Army evidently tolerates their rhythmic deficiencies because it needs their relatively scarce mathematical skills. Better to train a nerdy navigator with two left feet than a parade ground star who might have trouble figuring out where his plane is going. Pilots and bombardiers had to have 20-20 vision, but navigators can wear glasses.

One of the worst things about that Sunday parade is Monday. Every Monday morning we line up at the camp dry cleaners with our dust-streaked dress uniforms that look like vacuum cleaner dirt bags. We have to pay for that cleaning from our own cadet pay, $75 a month. The uniforms come back cleaned and pressed on Fridays, just in time for the next parade.

Free At Last On A Weekend Pass

The training equivalent of hell is the base policy that all cadets be confined to base for the first thirty days. Instead of getting a chance to wind down and have fun in town on weekends, we are drilled relentlessly to the point where we almost forget there is another life outside the base gates: a world of lovely young ladies in soft summer dresses, and dance bands and bars where raw recruits like us are said to be hailed as heroes.

You can imagine our high spirits when we finally pile aboard buses after those first thirty days, clutching our first passes. Destination? Hollywood! My new buddy, Mike Boomer and I head for a popular spot on La Cienega Boulevard in Los Angeles, "The Bar of Music."

We get a boisterous welcome from the bar crowd the moment we walk through the door in our cadet uniforms with propeller insignia on the lapels. It could hardly have been better if we'd captured and brought in Adolph Hitler, wriggling around in a gunnysack. Hollywood comedy actor B.S. Pulley beckons for us to join him at the bar, and buys us drinks.

Several World War I veterans in their forties and fifties come over to join the festivities, treating us as if we've just won World War II. Not a bad reception for a bunch of apprentice airmen who haven't even flown yet.

After a great dinner that thankfully did *not* include that Army mess hall delicacy, creamed chipped beef on toast, we finish off the evening jitterbugging with girls we meet at the famous Palladium. Then we head reluctantly back to camp in the wee hours so we won't get "gigged"—punished with loss of privileges—for missing that Sunday parade.

Next morning I oversleep and am roughly shaken awake in the pre-dawn darkness by an eager beaver cadet officer. As I struggle to sit up, bleary-eyed and fuzzy-headed, he says, "I'm puttin' you on report for being late to formation. What's your name, Mister?" Still half-asleep and resenting this officious character, I mumble "John Doe."

"How do you spell it?"

"D-O-E, sir."

He scribbles this down in his notebook and hurries away as if he can hardly wait to report me. I sneak out behind him, dressing on the run, hoping to blend into the rear ranks unnoticed. Out front, the beaver is officially tattling on me to an Air Force Lieutenant who seems to be having trouble concealing a smile. The Lieutenant turns to our formation and says, "One of you men who overslept this morning was asked to identify himself to this cadet officer, and he said his name was John Doe." There's a ripple of laughter from my comrades. "Would that cadet step forward and give us his real name?" Since I am now awake and in full possession of my senses, I do not step forward to identify myself, and the matter is quickly dropped.

Sgt. Bauman Doesn't Love Me

Our class nemesis is a regular Army drill instructor with little fondness for flyboys. He sports a bristly butch haircut and a scowl that could curdle milk.

"My name is Sergeant Bauman," he says after we fall into formation to listen up. "It's my job while you're here to turn you sorry-assed college types into soldiers. You'll make me proud or I'll make you sorry. Is that clear?"

In all fairness, I must admit that Sgt. Bauman had the gift of absolute clarity. I understood him instantly, perhaps because he never spoke to me directly without leaning within three inches of my ear.

One day he is maneuvering us up, down and all around, like a set of toy soldiers. "Column left, harrch! Column right, harrch! To the rear, harrch!" I can't help muttering to myself about why all this marching and rifle-twirling is necessary when us high-flying airmen will never be march-ing to ground battles or shooting rifles. Damned if Sgt. Bauman doesn't hear me. "Companeee, halt!" he shouts. "We got a wise ass mouthin' off in ranks!" He orders me to step out front for a public dressing down as "a sad sack who'd better shape up or be shipped out." It is a sharp and effective lesson in military realities, best expressed as "If you've got a problem, tell it to the chaplain."

Eventually I learn why all this Army performing-in-unison stuff is em-phasized so much. The military discovered long ago that men trained to instant, automatic obedience do a better job under the stress of combat. But I'm not nineteen yet and I know almost nothing about military life beyond the fact that everybody dresses exactly like everybody else. I am as wet behind the ears as it's possible to get without actually drowning.

I also have trouble meeting the perfectionist spit-and-polish demands of those hard-nosed cadet officers. They make frequent tent or barracks inspections while we recruits have to stand motionless at a respectful "parade rest" position beside our footlockers as they rummage through our belongings. Everything has to be just so. They'll bounce a quarter on our cots to make sure the blankets are properly taut. They look us up and down like judges at the Westminster Dog Show, checking our ties, collar insignia, and even the shininess of our brass belt buckles. Any cadet who doesn't pass muster will soon be denuding Idaho Russets behind the mess hall kitchen, or running penalty laps on the base exercise track.

Time To Relax

Whenever we have some free time I head for the day room with my comrades to feed coins into the jukebox. I blow all my small change playing favorite tunes of the day such as Freddie Slack's "Cow Cow

Boogie," bluesy vocals by the great Herb Jeffries, and the Andrews Sisters singing anything from "Don't Sit Under the Apple Tree" to "Rum and Coca-Cola."

These are the golden days of Swing. My favorite bandleaders are Glenn Miller, Benny Goodman, Tommy Dorsey and Artie Shaw. Sadly, Glenn Miller, who became an Army Major, was lost over the English Channel after D-day when his plane mysteriously disappeared while en route to entertain the troops in France. Reports suggested his plane might have been brought down by friendly fire.

Easily the biggest entertainment event while I'm training at Santa Ana is the appearance of the most popular female vocalist of this era, Dinah Shore. She performs on a small outdoor stage the size of a boxing ring, surrounded by hundreds of cheering, clapping cadets. I am right up front as she sings her biggest hits, such as "Shoo-Fly Pie" and "He's My Guy."

After three months at Santa Ana, I've actually been transformed into some semblance of military usefulness. Most importantly, I've learned who rates a salute, who doesn't, and why. I'm also in the best physical shape ever, after being run into total exhaustion on laps around the track by the Army's fitness fanatics. Daily calisthenics have also added weight to my non-fat frame, as well as muscles that can actually be seen by the naked eye. I am no hunk, but neither am I still that 120-pound beanpole that barely passed the weight minimum for his height. I squeaked through by gorging on half-a-dozen bananas before getting on the scales. If there's such a thing as banana breath, I must've had it for days.

Now that I've made it through pre-flight, it's time to follow that dream of becoming a fighter pilot like my RAF heroes in their Spitfires. Orders come through shipping me to Thunderbird Field in Arizona to start primary flight training. Mike gets his orders too, but he'll be going to bombardier school in New Mexico. We say goodbye, hoping to meet again on down the training road, and perhaps fly together overseas. Fate does eventually reunite us through combat, but in a most unexpected way.

CHAPTER THREE

TAKING OFF IN ARIZONA

The original Thunderbird Field in Arizona was the size of a postage stamp compared to modern military air bases and airports, but it played a major role in training the pilots who flew to victory in World War II. It occupied only a square mile of desert, built with private funds just months before Pearl Harbor.

Why private funds? Because Congress had refused to fund the massive buildup of warplanes and airfields that Air Corps General "Hap" Arnold knew were urgently needed by America.

After the Congressional rebuff, Gen. Arnold appealed for financial help to the Hollywood film stars of the day including Janet Gaynor, Jimmy Stewart, Henry Fonda and Hoagy Carmichael, as well as various business leaders. They give more than $1,000,000, an enormous sum at that time, to build this field where more than 16,000 Air Corps cadets learn to fly by war's end.

I arrive at Thunderbird in midsummer of 1942, during what feels like a heat wave. Arizona in midsummer *is* a heat wave. The very next morning I'm out there in the sizzling sun on a shimmering runway, ready for my first flying lesson in a PT-17 Stearman biplane.

The Stearman was ideal for novice pilots. Simple, rugged and extremely stable, it had two open cockpits, fabric-covered wooden wings, single-leg landing gear and a 220-hp, 7-cylinder radial engine. At a cruising speed of 100 miles per hour, it was in no danger of breaking the sound barrier.

I'd flown only once before, as an excited five-year-old in Cleveland, Ohio. My dad laid out five big bucks for me to join him sightseeing aboard a Ford tri-motor passenger plane.

Henry Ford had begun production of this remarkable all-metal aircraft just two years before in 1926 to encourage development of a whole new aviation travel industry. The third engine was his idea to create additional reliability, and thus encourage wary travelers to go by air. The public nicknamed his plane "The Tin Goose." This was in homage to Ford's "Tin Lizzie," the mass-produced Model T car that transformed road travel and modern life forever.

What a thrill it is for my dad and me as this magnificent flying machine passes very close to the Civic Center. My little stomach does a couple of loops as I look down the side of a skyscraper and can actually feel how high up we are.

Nearly 14 years later, here at Thunderbird, I'm anxious but fairly confident as I climb into the rear cockpit of a bright yellow Stearman. I figure I'm already a skilled car driver, totally at home on the road. How much harder can piloting be? I'm about to find out that there's a big difference between the skills required for driving in two dimensions, and flying in three.

Strapping myself in the back seat and adjusting my Snoopy-style helmet and goggles, I give the civilian instructor a thumbs up. He revs the engine to full throttle and releases the brakes. The little trainer biplane surges forward, rolls down the runway at gathering speed and lifts into the air. What a sensation in an open cockpit! The runway drops out from under us. As we rise ever higher above the earth, the feeling of rapid movement gradually melts away. At altitude it feels as if the plane is hardly moving, suspended in Arizona's brilliant and cloudless blue sky.

The instructor's voice crackles through the earphones: "Take the stick and keep us straight and level." The straight part is easy. Keeping level at the same time isn't. Anxious to do my best—too anxious—I'm like a deer hunter with buck fever. The plane keeps bobbing up and down, obeying one over-correction after another. "Hold it level!" the instructor shouts. "Level!" Turns aren't easy either. I need to finish an aerial turn by leveling out, not by letting the yoke slide through my fingers as I would a steering wheel in an earth-bound Chevy. If I don't level out like an eagle, I'll end up circling like a buzzard. So here I am, staggering and careening around the sky, trying to get the hang of it. The last thing I need is something else to think about, but that's what I get. Now my instructor wants me to keep swiveling my head to look around as pilots must to make sure no other planes are above, below, ahead, behind, to the left or right, ascending, descending, or turning into you or away. Putting all this together is like rubbing my stomach with one hand and patting my head with the other. It's a good thing drivers don't have to do all this swiveling, which literally is a pain in the neck. Fortunately a car driver isn't in a combat situation, worrying about hostiles sneaking up on his tail, unless it's rush hour on the freeway. The lesson ends with an abrupt, "That's enough for today." The instructor takes over, turns us back toward the base, and sets the plane down like a feather. Then he climbs out, says he'll see me the same time tomorrow, and walks off. I tell myself there's always tomorrow and I'll do better, but it's not a promising beginning.

By now the temperature is blazing at well over a hundred degrees. I head for the dayroom to escape the oven outside, get a cold drink and relax. My nerves are twanging like banjo strings, and I'm worried about my so-so performance. I'm all too aware that the Air Corps is "washing out" (flunking) anybody who doesn't show a natural aptitude for flying. Although the War Department is racing to build a huge air force, like those of both Nazi Germany and Japan, almost overnight, it has a tremendous pool of volunteers to choose from. There's no time to train anybody with average abilities. You'd better have "the right stuff." That's why cadets who've already had some pilot training in civilian life have a real edge over the rest of us.

"Red"

The dayroom feels at least 30° cooler than the sizzling airstrip. I grab a coke from the machine and sink down into a sofa. Moments later, a lanky, red-headed cadet in green flight overalls comes by and says "How're ya doing?' "OK," I say, too depressed to make small talk. He sits down at the piano nearby and begins to play one of my favorite instrumentals, "Autumn Nocturne." Hey, he is good! I let go of my worries for the time being and concentrate on enjoying this cadet's way with a piano. As he finishes the melody, I ask if he's a professional musician.

"I guess you could say that," he says. "Before the war came along, I was playing some lounge and bar gigs back in Dallas, and thinking of putting a little group together with some buddies."

17

He says he's been spending every cent he could get on flying lessons anyhow, so he decided to volunteer for the Army Air Corps. His class is just a few weeks ahead of mine.

His name? "Everybody calls me Red, What's yours?"

"Ray."

"How's it going for you, Ray?"

Wrong question. I pour out the whole dismal story about my first lesson.

"Well, most guys have a similar experience," he says. "They're so eager they try too hard. Those civilian instructors are tough. Just accept that fact, relax as much as you can, and you'll do better."

Well, he ought to know. By the time he plays a few more tunes, I'm feeling more relaxed. Finally he glances at his watch and says he has to go to class. "I come here to practice about this time every day," he says. "C'mon by if you can make it, and I'll play whatever you like."

After Red's comforting encouragement, I actually do feel more optimistic the next morning when I report to the flight line. Unfortunately the instructor isn't any happier. We practice turns and end up practicing a stall when he cuts the engine. Once we're back on the ground, I'm hoping he will give me some idea of how I'm doing. But all he says is "See you tomorrow."

Red is already in the dayroom, noodling at the piano as I come in. He looks up with a welcoming smile. "How did it go today, Ray?"

"Oh, about the same," I say. "How about you?"

"Man, it was a good day," Red says, grinning from here to there. "A really *good* day. Guess what?"

"What?"

"I soloed!"

"That's terrific! Congratulations, Red!" I'm really happy for him, seeing how elated he is, but I can't help envying him as well. Soloing means he has survived that first big hurdle and is on his way to being a pilot. After finishing primary, he'll most likely go on to earn his silver wings. Once a student makes it through the next step, basic training, and goes on to advanced training, he must be carefully re-evaluated on check rides with other instructors before he can be washed out.

As for Red, I'd never heard such happy music as our new "soloist" plays this afternoon. Dixieland, Ragtime, Boogie Woogie, you name it. Red is on a roll! A bunch of us cadets gather around the piano as if we're in a big city lounge, listening to a headliner. He is that good.

18

Bad News and More Bad News

Next morning as I take off again with the instructor, I remember Red's comforting words. I feel more confident about flying that Stearman. Maybe I'll make it after all. But my poker-faced tutor still seems unimpressed. When the lesson ends, he hops out of the cockpit and walks away without a word. I don't sleep well that night. Next morning I dawdle through breakfast, barely eating a few bites of scrambled eggs before going out to the flight line to check the bulletin board. There it is, the doomsday list of classmates being washed out and sent back to Santa Ana for reclassification. Halfway down the list, my name leaps out at me. Even though I'm not surprised, the blunt finality of it hits me hard. My dream of wearing pilot's wings is over. I'm finished—out the door. I've never wanted anything so badly, and now it will never happen. Hot tears start welling up. I hurry away, not wanting other cadets to see me like this.

Back in the empty barracks, I throw myself face down on my cot and surrender to racking sobs. This is the first real failure of my life and it hurts something awful. What can I say to Mom and Dad, or my kid brother? What will my friends back at the Examiner think? I don't know which feels worse, the shame or the heartbreak. Finally I regain control of myself, wash the tears away and set out for the dayroom. I want to say goodbye to Red and wish him well in basic training. He's not there yet, so I grab a coke and sit down by the piano to wait for him. A couple of cadets that I recognize as Red's classmates come in, so I ask if they know whether Red is on his way. They look at each other, and then back at me. One says, "You haven't heard?"

"Heard what?"

"He was practicing landings this morning – and crashed."

"Oh, no! Was he badly hurt? Is he in the hospital?"

"He was killed."

I have a hard time grasping those terrible words. It can't be. Not Red! Somehow I manage to make it back to the barracks. All I can think of is the shocking abruptness of Red's death and the tragic waste of such a promising life. His loss makes death and its close presence among us a vivid, chilling reality. The war is growing in intensity all over the globe, and I realize as never before that thousands more of us young Americans like Red will probably die in combat before our lives have really begun.

CHAPTER FOUR
A WASHOUT
GETS HIS GROOVE BACK

Flunking out of pilot training is the biggest disappointment of my life, and I don't have a clue how to deal with it. I just sit there on the train heading back to California, looking out the window but not seeing anything, marinating in misery. My family doesn't know for weeks what's happened at Thunderbird Field because I can't bring myself to write home about it. Arriving back at Santa Ana Army Air Base, I report to the reclassification officer to discuss my future, if any, with the Air Corps. He treats me with kind consideration. He's had to deal with a lot of derailed and depressed cadets like me who just didn't make it in pilot training. Leafing through papers in my file, he notes that I originally qualified for training in navigation or bombardier school as well as pilot training.

"Would you like to continue with flight training, or would you rather transfer out to the Army ground forces? They're looking for qualified men like yourself for anti-tank service."

"I'd rather stay with the Air Corps, sir. I'd like to go to navigation school."

"Well, that's a problem. They don't have room for new trainees right now. How about becoming a bombardier? I can send you to bombardier school in Roswell, New Mexico immediately."

Bombardier school was a distant third on my list. I'd much rather be a navigator, learning a skill of value in peacetime as well as war. But obviously that hope has faded away.

"That would be fine, sir."

He smiles and picks up a note on his desk. "One thing more. The Red Cross has tracked you down, and wants you to call your mother."

"Yes, sir." It was really embarrassing to hear this from the officer, but I'd been thinking only of myself. It will feel good talking to mom. I'm ashamed I haven't written her since I washed out.

"Very well," says the officer, rising from his chair to shake my hand. "We'll cut your orders to bombardier school in Roswell, New Mexico right away. Good luck." Somehow just knowing that something positive is happening begins to lift my bleak mood. It's time to put aside those fantasies about being a fighter pilot, suck it up and go where the Air Corps wants me to serve.

Shhhh! It's a Secret!

Back in the 1880's, Roswell was a typical little New Mexico town in Apache Indian country on the old Chisholm Trail. Cowhands on a cattle drive could stop to wet their dusty throats with all the liquor they could guzzle, followed by hell raising as a chaser. Some sixty years later, in 1940, wildcatters struck oil in Roswell and transformed it into a boomtown. It's very much on a wartime footing when my fellow cadets and I arrive at Roswell Army Air Base. Training is hush-hush because it involves learning to drop bombs by using the top-secret Norden bombsight. It is one of America's most highly treasured secrets, making possible the strategic high altitude bombing campaign against Nazi Germany. It will eventually be used by a new B-29 Superfortress bomber, the Enola Gay to drop the atomic bomb on Hiroshima to defeat Japan and hasten the end of World War II.

The Norden is one of the most complicated mechanical analog computers ever assembled. It is a whirring maze of gyros, motors, gears, mirrors, levers and a powerful telescope. It can calculate the very instant to release a bomb from an altitude of 21,000 feet and hit 95% to 100% of its targets—under practice conditions, that is. In combat, a bomber has to hold a straight and level course long enough for the bombsight to line itself up correctly before "bombs away." These final moments are the most dangerous of any mission, the time when black clouds of exploding flak shells and swarms of enemy fighters suddenly appear to shoot you down or blow you up. It takes tremendous concentration to keep flying straight and level under fire, no matter what. Again and again instructors drive home the point that the success of any mission depends on the bombardier's skills.

After three months of training, we are rewarded with Army commissions. As Commissioned Officers we now have the authority to give orders to all men of lesser ranks, and rate salutes from them as well. Being elevated from a lowly cadet to a commissioned status may not sound like much to civilians, but in the military it's like being a mortal invited to join the gods on Olympus. With bars on our shoulders, we are now military gods ourselves.

Surprise, Surprise!

We expect to ship out soon for advanced crew training and then to fly a bomber overseas to a theater of war, but, that's not in the Air Corps plans for me and about a half-dozen other grads. We've been chosen to go on to navigation school to earn a second pair of wings. This is quite a surprise, but officials explain that dual-rated bombardier-navigators will be needed for those huge new B-29 bombers when they start flying the longest missions of the war to Japan.

When we brand new 2nd Lieutenants arrive for navigation studies in Hondo, Texas, cadet classmates salute us. That feels good! But despite our glamorous new uniforms and silver wings, we are the same girl-crazy young guys as they are. We all want nothing more than to spend every weekend cavorting with those beautiful babes in San Antonio, that serviceman's paradise just thirty miles down the road.

Our base at Hondo in the humid south Texas plains is no resort. Its tar-papered, one-story classrooms are like sweat lodges. Flying high in cooler air to practice actual navigation feels great after all those steamy hours down below in class, hunched over Mercator charts as we are taught to plot a course from anywhere to anywhere else. The charts were created by a Flemish cartographer named Mercator nearly four centuries ago, in 1569. Navigators still use them because they convert our spherical earth into a two-dimensional flat plane to simplify plotting courses on paper.

As a group, navigation students are nerdier than either pilots or bombardiers, and understandably so. We have to master several sets of skills ranging from simple pilotage—visual navigation from town to town—to advanced celestial navigation, shooting the stars with sextants to plot our

A page from the Air Corps operations manual for the top secret Norden Bombsight.

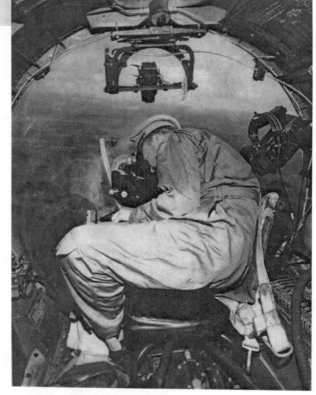

Using the Norden Bombsight.

progress like navigators at sea.

We also study dead reckoning, the art of finding your way from your last known position to your destination when you can't see anything above or below in heavy weather. It involves calculations based on the last known winds aloft, and how they affect your course and ground speed.

As a navigator I'll be the only crewmember manning a desk instead of a gun. Besides keeping track of where we are at all times, I must be ready in case of trouble to tell the pilot immediately what course can get us home or to the nearest emergency landing field.

Wild And Crazy Guys

Every Saturday night, after a long and exhausting week's studies in class and aloft, we student officers have the privilege of going to San Antonio with weekend passes. We turn into wild and crazy guys with extra flight pay in our pockets and a freewheeling urge to blow every last cent on dates, dancing and romancing. Whatever else its claims to fame are, Texas is home to some of the most beautiful women I ever hope to see. They're everywhere every weekend at taverns and dancehalls, and they really sho' 'nuf cotton to us free-spending flyboys. There's even a hit song about us, "He Wears A Pair Of Silver Wings" on all the jukeboxes. We are hot stuff—or like to think we are. Brand new second Louies ride into town together every Saturday, crammed into a powerful '42 Mercury sedan, one of the last models to roll off the pre-war assembly lines. We chip in to pay for a standing reservation at a popular hotel downtown with a suite, a bar, and accommodations for those lucky enough to find a playmate in the weekend melee. After some jitterbugging to tunes at the top of the charts like "American Patrol," "String of Pearls" and "Chattanooga Choo-Choo" we take our dates to dinner. Then we try inveigling the girls to come up for drinks at our hotel suite where a non-stop party is always going on. Inveigling often succeeds because there are always fun-loving girls around who come to town with every intention of getting inveigled.

As you might imagine, it isn't easy after a weekend of revelry to face reveille on Monday mornings. We struggle out of our bunks well before classes start to go where our planes are parked, put on oxygen masks and inhale the pure stuff until our hangovers calm down and the mists clear from our minds. This has to happen before breakfast, so we can eat one. Once the miseries lift I am back at my studies, concentrating as if the world outside our base doesn't exist. Besides, I really enjoy the challenge of mastering aerial navigation. I give it my best.

A Happy Dilemma

When it comes time to graduate after several months of intensive air and ground classes, they present us student officers with *a second pair* of wings. That's a big thrill, but what are we supposed to do with them? Wear them both where wings normally go on the left chest? That looked awkward, oddly like a biplane. So, I try wearing one on each side when we go into town and am greeted by much older servicemen with double takes and hasty salutes. The gold bars on my shoulders tell them I am an officer, but they've obviously never, ever encountered anybody wearing *two* sets of wings. It was embarrassing for all concerned, so the next weekend I left the bombardier wings behind and wore the new navigator pair.

After receiving my navigator's wings I'm invited by the base staff to stay on as an instructor. Wow! That's tempting! I'd often thought in high school about teaching as a career and, if the war hadn't come along, I'd probably have gone on to pursue becoming an English professor because I love books and the English language. However, I turn the instructorship down because I feel my higher duty is to go overseas and fight for my country. Looking back, I realize that I might have contributed more to the war effort as an instructor than I could by flying missions. But, try explaining that to the gung-ho, idealistic youth I was then.

Meanwhile, a decision I didn't make seals what I will do in the war. I'd been trained specifically for the new B-29s to serve on long flights to bomb Japan, but now the 8th Air Force in England is suffering heavy casualties in the skies over Europe and replacements are badly needed. So—surprise again! I'm ordered to advanced training in B-24 Liberator bombers which will soon be joining the Mighty 8th Air Force in its ferocious, make-or-break struggle against Hitler's Luftwaffe in the skies over Occupied Europe.

CHAPTER FIVE

READYING FOR WAR

When flying in combat, your life depends on every man in the crew doing his job. The better they are, the better your chances of ever coming home again. A crew is like an infantry squad in one major respect, a group of buddies who fight together and share a common fate. I meet the crew I'll navigate for at Gowen Army Air Base in Boise, Idaho. Gowen is a staging area for assembling bomber crews and assigning them and their planes to heavy bombardment groups for final training before going off to war. I feel as if I won a lottery when I find out that my pilot-to-be, Peter Abell has been a senior instructor on the Boise flight line with hundreds of flying hours under his belt. I figure flying with him will be like having a guardian angel at the controls.

Well, Pete turns out to be a terrific guy, someone you can always count on in a tight spot—but his wings don't make him an angel. He's a good time Charlie, a frat boy from Northern California who's always joking around and spending every off-duty moment chasing women. As a pilot, he has "the right stuff." Pete also has the right stuff for his avocation, the hot pursuit of attractive dates. To look at him, you might wonder how he does it. He's of average height, about 5'10", and a little too chubby to rate as a hunk. But he has merry blue eyes, blond curly hair, and a gentle way with women that puts them at their ease. Since I'm four years younger and obviously inexperienced in Pete's specialty, he never ever asks me to join him cruising the bars of Boise on a weekend pass. He seems to know instinctively what to do when, and he's the guy to do it. I remember a knockout blonde named Marie who worked at the lunch counter in the base mess hall. Pete put such a whammy on her that when we are ordered to Pocatello, Idaho to train with other crews, Marie quits her job to follow him. Women live with far less scrutiny of their behavior during the war, and anxiety about female sexuality becomes a public concern. Females who flout conventional morals are called "Victory Girls," "Khaki-Whackies" or "Good Time Charlottes."

Pete likes to boast that he has assembled the best crew anywhere. As a senior instructor he got first pick of incoming personnel when he chose to go overseas. "I went through all your training records to find you guys," he told me. Walter "The Bomber" Yerkes was named a bombardier of the month at training school. A tall, quiet eighteen-year-old from rural Pennsylvania, Walt is a talented perfectionist who always pounds the target on our practice bombing runs.

Co-pilot Tom Campbell, a shy and soft-spoken Iowan, is qualified to command a bomber of his own, but prefers to fly in the right-hand seat beside Pete instead. I make the crew after Pete learns I could have been an instructor but chose combat duty just as he has.

All the enlisted crewmen are rated outstanding in their specialties. Pete stole our engineer, Master Sergeant Donald E. Caton, right off the flight line at Boise. Don is a stocky, ruddy-faced regular Air Corps man with a crew cut and a confident way with aircraft innards that is awesome. There doesn't seem to be anything that he can't fix on the ground or jury-rig in the air to keep us flying. Radio operator Tech/Sgt. Donald E. Watts, who also mans the top turret gun, is another expert. So are waist gunners Sergeants Lonnie E. Reeves and Allen Alford, ball turret gunner Walter W. Merriam and tail turret gunner Sergeant Ned A. Dougherty. All these sharp-eyed young men scored consistently high at tracking and blasting fast moving aerial targets.

After being assigned to crews and becoming acquainted with our new B-24 Liberator bomber, we are transferred to Pocatello, Idaho to begin individual practice flights all over the country. The B-24 is a dependable aircraft with a faster cruising speed and longer range than the better-known B-17 Flying Fortress. It can fly 300 miles per hour at 30,000 feet, carry 8,000 pounds of bombs and has an operational range of 2,290 miles. It's so versatile that it also serves as a reconnaissance aircraft, submarine bomber and aerial ferry for transporting pilots and personnel

**Ray at the
Los Angeles
Examiner.**

**Just before
going overseas.**

BACK ROW: Capt. Peter Abell, pilot; 2nd Lt. RAY PARKER, navigator; Sgt. Walter Merriam, ball turret gunner; 2nd Lt. Walter Yerkes, bombardier; 2nd Lt. Tom Campbell, co-pilot.

FRONT ROW: Sgt. Allen Alford, waist gunner; M/Sgt. Donald E. Caton, flight engineer; Tech/Sgt. Donald E. Watts, radio operator; Sgt. Ned A. Dougherty, tail turret gunner; and Sgt. Lonnie E. Reeves, waist gunner.

across the North Atlantic. This heavily armed craft is eventually credited with helping the Allies to take and maintain control of the vital sea-lanes.

Flying Off to Dreamland

All goes well at Pocatello until one night I doze off on a long distance flight while I'm supposed to be shooting the stars with my sextant for practice in celestial navigation. Pete's voice in my earphones suddenly jolts me awake. "Hey, Parker! Where are we?"

Pete's been flying the last heading I gave him nearly an hour ago, and hasn't seen my head pop up lately in the star sighting bubble. Naturally he is wondering what I'm doing. Terribly embarrassed, I mutter something about "updating our position" and begin shuffling through likely maps, trying for a quick match up to what I can make out in the darkness below. Wherever we are, we aren't supposed to be there. Finally I recognize a unique multi-channeled stretch of river gleaming faintly in the moonlight up ahead. It's the Platte in Nebraska, well beyond our assigned flight route!

I take a deep breath to calm down, and then get on the intercom and say casually, "It's time to turn around, Pete. Do a 180." So while he swings the plane back onto a reverse course, I click off several star shots, plot our position and give Pete a corrected heading for Pocatello. I never do confess to that nap, knowing he'd have ribbed me mercilessly for the rest of the war. He'd have thought up some wacko nickname for me as he did for other goof-ups, something appropriate like Larry Lost, Nappy the Navigator, or Possum Parker.

Our Squadron Commander Is…Jimmy Stewart!

Soon our crew is declared ready to join the newly formed 445th Heavy Bombardment Group for final training as a Group in Sioux Falls, South Dakota before going overseas. Imagine our surprise when we learn that the commanding officer of our 703rd squadron will be the world-famous film star, Captain Jimmy Stewart! Pete had met Stewart as a fellow instructor at Gowen. Stewart had wanted to go overseas but had been assigned to train other pilots instead. After six frustrating months of this he makes an appeal to his commanding officer, Colonel "Pop" Arnold. Stewart tells "Pop" he wants a combat assignment but fears he will be

Jimmy Stewart,
Ray's Commanding Officer.

Jimmy and Ray
united after the war.

kept stateside as an instructor. Evidently no one wants to take responsibility for sending this superstar overseas to risk his life. Arnold sees Stewart's determination and decides to help. He telephones his friend, Col. Robert Terrell, who is forming the 445th. Col. Terrell agrees to take on Capt. Stewart as a squadron operations officer. That's how the actor begins his distinguished service in the Eighth Air Force. Our crew is lucky to serve in his first combat command.

As the air war rages on, Stewart becomes recognized by the high command as one of the finest combat officers in Air Force history. He survives twenty combat missions, winning two Distinguished Flying Crosses, four Air Medals and the French Croix de Guerre with Palm. He rises to become a full Colonel as Chief of Staff of the Second Air Division, which includes all the B-24s of the Eighth Air Force. After the war he serves in the U.S. Army Air Forces Reserve, reaching the rank of a Brigadier General in 1957 and retiring in 1967.

At Sioux Falls Air Force Base, our crews practice flying in close formation as a group. This tactic, which earlier combat crews had to learn the hard way in the skies over Nazi-occupied Europe, is crucial to concentrate our firepower for fending off fighter attacks. Stragglers or crippled aircraft that can't keep up are pounced upon by the enemy and sent down in flames. We practice day and night missions, using dead reckoning and celestial navigation while keeping strict radio silence to avoid giving our positions away.

One of our scariest practice missions is a night flight in steadily worsening weather. We're already being buffeted by a thunderstorm when a crewman on the intercom shouts, "Look at the props! What the hell is that?" We see a ghostly, truly eerie phenomenon—all four propellers and the edges of the wing are aglow. "It's called St. Elmo's fire," says Pete. "I've heard of it, but never seen it before. It happens sometimes during thunder storms." Weird as it was, I'll take St. Elmo's fire any time, compared to what happens a few weeks later.

Lightning Strikes

I'm at the parachute shack, waiting beside three other flyers to check out chutes for a practice flight. We're standing at the counter near a wood stove. I remember glancing out the window as a bolt of lightning hits a few hundred yards away with an ominous crash and earth-shaking rumble. "Looks like the storm's getting worse," I say. "Maybe we shouldn't go up today."

Suddenly the whole shack lights up with a blinding flash. I feel a flood of paralyzing electricity surging through my body as I crumple to the wooden floor. Dazed and disoriented, I manage to stagger back to my feet and see the other men, who were closer to the stove, lying sprawled on the floor, unconscious. A lightning bolt that traveled down through the stove's chimney flue flattened us all. The parachute counter man, untouched, just stands there with his mouth agape, transfixed by the sight.

"Call an ambulance!" I yell. He doesn't move. I grab the phone sitting in front of him and call the base hospital. The guys on the floor are starting to groan and roll around. Heavy rain is battering the windows in an immense, bucketing downpour. Within minutes an ambulance, siren wailing, pulls up outside. I help the driver carry out the three barely conscious men on stretchers. As we load the last one aboard the driver says, "Get in." "Oh, I'm okay," I reply. He says, "Yeah? Feel the left side of your face." I do—and my hand comes away covered with blood. Suddenly I feel weak and shaky. I crawl into the rear of the ambulance and bend my head down between my knees to avoid passing out. Despite all the blood, my injury turns out to be little more than a gash in my earlobe where I'd hit the floor.

The men who absorbed most of the bolt are hospitalized for weeks, lucky to be alive. Two had the zippers down the sides of their flying overalls welded shut by the bolt. The third had the soles ripped right off his shoes, leaving black scorch marks on the flesh where nail heads had been. I am so rattled by the experience that for months afterwards the sound of a distant thunderclap is enough to make me want to dive under the nearest bed.

Farmers and Haymakers

Training is intense, day and night. To relax between practice missions, we either go into Sioux Falls or cross the South Dakota state line for all the rowdy excitement at a roadhouse where farmers in bib overalls dance with their wives and girl friends. Often a night ends abruptly in dance floor fistfights between farmers while we outsiders retreat to a neutral corner at the bar. We never do find out what those folks are fighting about. They seem neighborly enough until they tank up on beer and bourbon. Then it's best to leave the floor, or risk dancing right into a roundhouse haymaker intended for some other boozy belligerent.

Ready for Battle

After weeks of diligent practice the 445th is finally pronounced battle-ready. By this time, November of 1943, the 8th Air Force in England is taking very heavy casualties during its daylight missions over Europe. Hitler's Luftwaffe is putting up ferocious resistance. The Eighth urgently needs reinforcements and replacements to carry on its strategic mission of destroying Nazi war-making facilities such as tank and aircraft factories, munitions depots, oil refineries and railroad marshalling yards. We are destined to fly in the biggest, thousand-plane raids of the war—and pay the price for doing it.

CHAPTER SIX

GOING OVERSEAS

We are ferrying our bomber across the South Atlantic, on our way to England to join the air war against Nazi Germany. Our crew is on high alert as we skim low over the water to avoid being spotted by Nazi U-boats that are known to lie in ambush out here with their deck guns ready to blast us from the skies. It is mid-November, 1943. The young Captain who briefs us before takeoff from Natal in Brazil this morning makes sure we understand that this flight is no piece of cake. "Ascension Island is 1,437 miles from here, all by itself in the middle of the South Atlantic, and it's only eight miles wide," he says. "The British who operate our refueling station on the island broadcast a navigational beam, but you can't rely on it because enemy subs have been known to send out fake beams to lure our planes off course. If that happened, you'd probably run out of gas and crash in the ocean." Pete, sitting next to me in the steamy and stifling briefing room, whispers, "You'd better find us that island!"

The briefing officer continues: "We lost a bomber just yesterday. No idea what happened. It disappeared somewhere between here and Ascension. We've lost several others in the past few months as well. Sometimes it's mechanical failure, sometimes it's enemy action, and sometimes, like yesterday, we just don't know. So fly low, stay alert—and good luck."

Yeah, good luck! That little talk felt like a cold shower. Until this morning, the journey begun at our advanced training base in Sioux Falls, South Dakota had been a pleasant adventure. We'd spent the past few days flying from Iowa to southern Florida, then on to San Juan in Puerto Rico, then to equatorial Georgetown, British Guiana, and finally across the Brazilian jungle to our jump-off point here at Natal, on the eastern bulge of Brazil.

Sweating Out A Landing

It's nearly eight hours since we took off, and we are 1,300 miles out to sea. We have another half hour or more to go before we can hope to spot that all-important speck of land in the middle of the vast South Atlantic Ocean. I can feel the tension ratcheting up in the plane as each crewman keeps scanning the horizon, reporting nothing but water in all directions. We know there's nothing out here, but hours and hours of seeing such vast stretches of empty ocean and no signs of life is unsettling all the same. It feels as if we're not really getting anywhere. I am continually checking the drift meter, sighting down onto the ocean waves to measure the winds aloft which affect our heading and air speed. A change in wind direction must be factored in whenever it happens so we won't be carried off course. Assuming we maintain a cruising speed of 170 mph, the flight will take 8 hours and 27 minutes. Even though it's going well, I can't help sweating it out. I've calculated what navigators call "the point of no return," that time when we won't have enough fuel left to turn back to Brazil if trouble strikes. As we pass that fateful point, I think of what that briefing officer said. We could die out here in this immense nowhere if anything goes wrong.

It's late afternoon as Pete's voice comes through my earphones with the same question he's been asking on and off all day: "How're we doing, Parker?"

"We have another half hour or so to go," I say. "I'll give you a heads-up as soon as we're close enough to see something." Radio operator Watts is monitoring the island's radio beam, and the heading I've calculated seems to agree with his reading, so that's a good thing.

As our plane approaches that make-or-break moment when we will or won't see Ascension Island coming into view, I take another good look around in the navigator's bubble. There's still nothing to see but water and a small group of low-lying clouds ahead, slightly off to the left. As

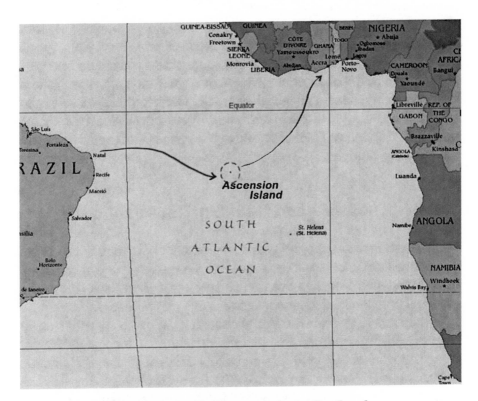

South Atlantic flight en route to England.
1,437 miles of travel from Natal,
Brazil to Ascension Island,
then another 1,357 miles to Accra, Ghana.

Wideawake Airfield on Ascension Island.

Pete sees my head pop up in the bubble he comes on the intercom and says, "I still don't see anything, Parker. Do you?"

"I don't see any land yet, Pete, but it figures to be under those clouds," I tell him. If it isn't, I'd rather not think about that. Pete banks the plane a few degrees left, heading directly toward the cloud formation. Every man on board is straining to see—and then—there it is! "Whaddya know," says Pete. "We made it!" I feel so buoyant with relief that I could float right out of my flying boots.

The Loneliest Island In The Atlantic

Rocky and barren, Ascension Island is a roost for hundreds of sea birds. Now a small group of buildings comes into view, near a runway that rises up and then slants down across a volcanic peak. Pete banks the plane and turns onto the final approach, coming in for a flawless landing on the 6,000-foot runway. It feels like a roller coaster as we roll up and then down to a stop. British airmen in blue uniforms stride out to welcome us. Before taking us to dinner they give us a proud tour of their hydroponics gardens in greenhouses. Dating back to the 1930's, hydroponics is the science of growing plants in a liquid nutrient solution rather than in soil. With hydroponics, perfect tomatoes can be grown in a desert or the middle of winter. I was impressed with how the Brits could make themselves at home on this bleak volcanic rock. It's no island paradise.

The United States Government built the airstrip and its facilities, "Wideawake Field," during the war by arrangement with Her Majesty's Government. The airfield's name comes from the Wideawake bird, a sooty tern that nests there. From 1943 to 1945, more than 25,000 U.S. planes come here to refuel en route to the North African, Middle East and European theatres of war (I have to assume they solved that navigation beam problem to accomplish such an enormous airlift). I try my best to sleep that night, but my mind keeps revving away. It feels so surreal to be smack in the middle of the South Atlantic, on one of the remotest islands on earth.

Heading For The Gold Coast

The next morning, with our plane and ourselves refueled, we take off up and down that roller coaster runway and swing onto a heading for

Accra, the capitol of Ghana on the Gold Coast of Africa. It will be another marathon 1,357-mile flight, lasting eight hours at cruising speed, but with far less tension because it's so much easier to find a continent than a remote slab of rock like Ascension Island.

Soon after we make landfall late that afternoon at Accra, at a tropical airfield fringed by palm trees, we are tempted to take on another passenger. A handsome black twelve-year-old boy in khaki shorts and a T-shirt begs us in very passable English to let him join us as our servant. "I have no family," he says. "I take good care of you." Tom produces a D-bar chocolate ration from his flight jacket pocket and gives it to the boy, but Pete has to tell this appealing youngster that there is no way we can take him aboard a military aircraft. The boy understands, but he's there the next morning, waving a teary goodbye as Pete revs up for takeoff. We set a course for Marrakech in Southwestern Morocco, our last fueling stop before heading on to England.

The flight north over western Africa is uneventful, but a culture shock awaits us as we arrive at Marrakech on the edge of the Mediterranean. Dozens of Arab women in white flowing dresses are lined up along the edges of the runway, greeting us by making a weird high-pitched sound called ululating with their tongues, and waving their raised skirts. What that skirt-waving business means we wouldn't know, but it's certainly an icebreaker. Before we can leave the plane, an American Sergeant comes aboard and surprises us by spraying the entire interior of the plane with DDT insecticide—including us! When we finally jump down onto the runway, we're puzzled to see Italian soldiers in uniform wandering everywhere. They are prisoners of war, so glad to be in American hands instead of fighting for the Germans that nobody bothers to pen them up. They spend their free-roaming hours happily doing whatever chores their captors assign to them.

Forbidden Fun in the Kasbah

The weather turns worse instead of better for several days, grounding all flights. Pete, Tom, Walt and I take advantage of this unexpected break by hitching rides into downtown Marrakech to go sightseeing. This ancient city, founded more than a thousand years ago by Arab warriors, looks more like a set for a French Foreign Legion movie. It's teeming with Arabs in long robes, dodging between horse-drawn carriages as they cross the busy main boulevard. We've been warned that American service-

41

men are forbidden to go into the native quarter because it's considered too dangerous. Naturally, a restriction like that makes Pete all the more eager to go. Silver-tongued rascal that he is, he persuades Tom and me to accompany him. Walt, the more sensible straight arrow, hitches a ride back to base instead. Private adventuring without the blessings of the authorities holds no allure for Walt. He is a more serious, by-the-book kind of guy.

The pilots and I set out for the Kasbah wearing holstered .45's that will come in handy in case of trouble. All service officers of WWII carry these formidable weapons for personal defense. My pistol is more for show to intimidate evildoers, since I know from firing range experience that I can't count on hitting a Sequoia with it. I would have preferred a Thompson sub machine gun, because I'd discovered in Tommy gun practice that I could spray a target area with a stream of bullets until I actually hit something.

Our foray into the native Kasbah quarter is a lot of fun. As for danger, not a single hashish-crazed fanatic wielding a scimitar springs out at us from ambush, as they did in movies of the Thirties like the classic "Beau Geste." Instead, we and our local cash are joyously welcomed by both merchants and entertainers at a crowded open-air market. We buy goat leather wallets, and tip a snake charmer who plays a flute-like instrument while a cobra comes swaying up out of a pottery bowl, another movies reminder. Afterwards we are approached by temptresses of the Kasbah who offer with rather erotic gestures to make their pleasures available. Pete waves these friendly damsels away. You've got to draw the line somewhere, preferably this side of trouble. Besides, it's time to hurry back to town in case the weather clears for a midnight flight to England.

CHAPTER SEVEN

TO ENGLAND
THE HARD WAY

After a week's delay we are finally cleared to take off for an all-night flight to England. Orders are to stay at least 100 miles out to sea from the coast of Spain because it is a dictatorship sympathetic to Nazi Germany. Spain was a training ground for Nazi Stuka dive-bombers during the Spanish Civil War. They bombed and strafed Spanish Republic soldiers and civilians as practice for conquering Europe. If our plane should go down in Spanish territory, we would surely be interned there for the rest of the war.

It is an unusually clear and moonlit night as we climb to cruising altitude. Our destination is Land's End, on the southwest tip of England. Radioman Watts homes in on a powerful navigation beam from Prestwick in Scotland while I track our progress with dead reckoning and star shots. The gunners are on alert in case German fighters come looking for us. The Germans know we're out here.

All goes well for an hour or so until our right outboard engine suddenly develops trouble. Pete shuts it down, feathering the prop to stop it rotating, and trimming the aircraft to balance the engine torque so it will keep us straight and level as we continue on course. Then comes more serious grief. An engine on the left wing quits running! This is truly bad news, because now we'll have trouble maintaining altitude. Pete trims the aircraft again to re-balance the torque and levels out. Then he comes on the intercom: "Parker! We're turning back. Give me a course to the nearest emergency field."

"Roger, Pete!" I check my charts. "There's a landing strip on the western Moroccan coast."

I hastily calculate the course and Pete banks around onto the new heading. Meanwhile crew chief Caton is trying to get that left engine going again. Then something totally unexpected happens, something that is supposedly impossible. The first engine that had been feathered suddenly runs away at full speed with a power surge that torques us over into a steep dive! We hurtle downward, plunging faster and faster toward the ocean. It's time for a miracle or we're done for. The plane keeps plummeting down, down, down until I can see the water rushing up at us in the moonlight, less than a thousand feet away. We're just seconds from certain death. But at the last possible, heart-stopping moment the runaway engine exhausts its fuel and the plane levels out. That was close! Pete tells me later that he, Tom and Sgt. Caton had all been hauling back on the controls together, straining with all their might to pull the nose up out of the dive.

Now we must hold altitude and stay aloft long enough to reach that landing strip. Radioman Watts alerts the emergency field. Workers on standby there will have to set out flare pots if we're to have a prayer of finding the airstrip in the darkness. Meanwhile our rough-running engines could quit at any moment. Somehow Pete keeps us airborne until we come in low over the coastline where the field is marked on the chart—but we can't see any flares! Pete makes another pass even lower, directly above the supposed landing area, but there are still no flare pots to guide us down. As we swing around a third time, several pots blaze up at last, outlining the strip. Pete banks gently to line up with the runway and sits the plane down gently between the flares like the terrific pilot he truly is. And that's the exact moment when one of the two remaining engines quits running! Had that happened sooner, we would have crashed. By the time we hop aboard an Army truck to ride back to the main base, Pratt & Whitney engine specialists are already reported en route to Marrakech from the USA to investigate how what shouldn't and couldn't have happened did happen. Meanwhile our plane is being trucked back to the base for complete refitting.

Cheating Death Again

It's an odd feeling when you really get the message that your life depends on the reliability of your aircraft, particularly when it's a land plane on a long night's journey over ocean waters. After our near-death spiral, it's reassuring a week later to have new engines that seem to be running perfectly as we begin our second attempt to reach England. Taking off at night from Marrakech is worrisome in any case because the runways are so close to the 3,000-foot peaks of the Atlas Mountains. Planes have to fly toward them while gaining altitude. If a pilot holds that heading too long in the darkness, he and his crew are doomed. A crew that took off the night before us did make that fatal error. We just happen to be driving by the base hospital as an ambulance arrives to unload their bodies wrapped in blood-soaked sheets.

When it's our turn to take off, Pete makes sure we miss those mountains, and Radioman Watts again homes in on that powerful directional beam from Prestwick in Scotland to guide our journey. All I have to do is keep track of our progress. Soon after dawn we come in right over our destination: Land's End in Cornwall, on the southwest coast of England. The landscape below us is a misty, incredibly green checkerboard of farms and countryside.

They're Not Babes, They're Lassies

After landing, we walk in to town to register at a nearby hotel. On the way, we see a group of four local lasses with arms linked as they stride along, singing this tune:

"Roll me over, in the clover,
"Roll me over, lay me down
And do it again,
"Now this is number one
"And my song has just begun,
"Roll me over, lay me down
"And do it again.
"Roll me over, in the clover,
"Roll me over, lay me down
"And do it again."

This racy ballad goes on for several verses, as so many old English ditties do. The girls go on as well down the road, leaving us with a warm glow and an earnest desire to get better acquainted. When we reach our seaside hotel for the night, we encounter what Prime Minister Winston Churchill meant when he said that Great Britain and the United States are "divided by a common language." It begins with the cheery young Miss at the hotel desk who asks us, "What time shall I knock you up in the morning?" We all do double takes on that one. Soon after, a lovely barmaid tells us a drink costs "two and six." She isn't asking for eight somethings; the bill is two shillings and sixpence.

It's time for lunch so we set out on foot again to find a nearby restaurant. I ask an English gentleman how many more blocks we have to go, and he looks mystified. "Blocks? What are blocks?" I tell him it's a way we Americans have of measuring distances between streets. "Oh," says he. "Well, the place you're seeking is just a tuppenny ride from here." Pointing to a road winding up a nearby hill, he says, "You deny yourself the first turn and take the second. You can't miss it." Now it's my turn to be mystified. I can just see myself after that tuppenny ride, whatever that is, standing on that first corner, wherever that is, denying myself a turn. We do find the hotel eventually, after a tuppeny ride's worth of walking while obliging townsfolk point the way. We all order the fish and chips, the chips being what Americans call French Fries. You could buy them anywhere in Britain at roadside stands, served wrapped in a newspaper.

Our New Home

Next morning we take off for our final destination, a former Royal Air Force airbase at the centuries-old little town of Tibenham, not far from Norwich in East Anglia. This entire region of southeastern England is like an enormous aircraft carrier, housing some 130 military airfields. Forty-two are homes for Eighth Air Force B-17 and B-24 Bombardment Groups such as ours, and 14 house our fighter escorts—our little brothers, the P-47 and P-51 Fighter Groups. After a short flight we land at Tibenham in flat farming country. The base has the usual runways, control and communications tower, repair hanger facilities and individual hardstands for parking our aircraft. Soon we are housed in Quonset hut versions of barracks and officers' quarters. There are also a mess hall, day room facilities, a small auditorium for intelligence briefings on missions, and an officers club where those crews not on alert for a mission can relax over a few pints of Guinness.

The town of Norwich is the place all our airmen go between missions, to meet girls and have fun at the town dancehall. American servicemen have already taught the British girls to jitterbug. To me, the spectacle of traditional British ballroom dancing is almost quaint, with the gentlemen holding their ladies at arm's length while taking long, swooping strides across the floor. British dancing seems more like ice-skating, and not much warmer. We Yanks have more cash in our pockets than English airmen do. Free spending Yanks are notorious among the Brits for plying their new girlfriends with gifts of nylons and other scarce items seldom found or even affordable in wartime Britain's shops. Inevitably, some Brits complain that Americans are "overpaid, oversexed and over here." Others predict that the biggest battle of the war will take place when British Eighth Army veterans return to find America's Eighth Army Air Force flyboys romancing their sweethearts.

Despite their tremendous wartime sacrifices, the British are great hosts. Their warmth and kindness make a lot of difference to us home-sick-Yanks. We are proud that they regard us as comrades in arms to the gallant young Brits and Canadians who fly the Spitfire and Hurricane fighters and Lancaster night bombers of the Royal Air Force and the Royal Canadian Air Force. Many Brits seek us out and personally thank us for coming to their aid in the darkest days of the war, after Hitler had conquered and enslaved most of Europe. The Brits still remember, and have been our staunchest ally to this day.

CHAPTER EIGHT

ENGAGING THE ENEMY

After arriving at Tibenham our crew spends a couple of weeks getting used to flying combat formation in crowded skies, and practicing landing with the aid of those amazing top-secret British radar "G" boxes I'd never heard of before that make it visually easy to guide our plane right down onto the runway in zero visibility. If only this new radar had the power to reach across the channel to our targets! Despite terrible weather our group commander, Col. Robert Terrell, has us flying combat missions in short order. The group flies seven missions in eighteen days. My crew gets its baptism of enemy fire just three days before Christmas, on December 22, 1943. I have trouble sleeping the night before because my mind keeps racing, wondering what the target will be, how heavily defended by fighters and artillery barrages that we have to fly through, and whether we'll be among the lucky ones who make it back in one piece.

Awakened around four a.m., I board a truck to the mess hall for a breakfast of real eggs and bacon, a rarity in this land of strict wartime rationing. Then I join all the other pilots, navigators and bombardiers assigned to this morning's mission in the briefing building, a small auditorium. I can feel the tension as every man in the room stares intently at an intelligence officer striding onstage. He's about to reveal where our target is and how rough the opposition is expected to be. He lifts a cover from a map of Western Europe, revealing a bright red piece of yarn that stretches from our base in East Anglia across the English Channel to Osnabruck, in Germany's highly industrialized Ruhr Valley. Veterans of earlier missions groan in dismay. They know all too well that we'll be facing massed batteries of as many as a thousand highly accurate anti-aircraft "flak" guns, as well as numerous fighter squadrons. It's a good bet that some of us will never return.

"Gentlemen," says the briefing officer, "your target is the center of the city."

It surprises me to hear this, knowing from history that European cities have grown for centuries from the inside out, with modern factories on the outskirts. If this is true of Osnabruck, there will be residential areas in our target zone. I'm not very comfortable with that idea. We Americans considered the Nazis' indiscriminate bombing of English civilians during the aerial Battle of Britain as barbaric. I had assumed we would be bomb-ing strictly strategic military targets to weaken the German war machine and thus shorten this global conflict. Unfortunately, bombing in broad daylight through overcast skies in the face of fierce resistance isn't all that accurate. Sometimes it takes several missions, at high cost in flyers' lives and aircraft, to cause major damage to key targets such as aircraft factories, ball bearing plants, railroad marshalling yards and oil fields. Even if factories are knocked out of production, the Germans go all-out to put them back on line in a relatively short time. Then we go back and hit them again.

After the intelligence officer tells us all he knows about today's target and its defenses, we expect heavy opposition, which usually means heavier casualties. It will certainly be no "milk run," as combat flyers de-scribe a mission when resistance is light or non-existent. As the briefing ends, we go off to separate meetings of pilots, bombardiers and naviga-tors to study the final details that affect our roles.

Near take-off time, we meet our crews at the individual plane parking areas called hard stands. Armorers working in the freezing darkness have already loaded each bomber with tons of high explosives. Ground crews have filled our gas tanks and checked the engines. With a maximum load of bombs and gasoline, everything has to be right the first time or we can crash on takeoff, and perhaps blow up.

I grab a heavy armored flak suit from a nearby bin for protection from the shrapnel that will soon be exploding all around us. Taking off at quick intervals, our 445th heavy bombardment group lumbers heavily into the sky. Leading the group is our own squadron commander, Major Jimmy Stewart. We assemble and fall in line with other groups jockeying for their assigned positions in a thunderous aerial parade of several hundred aircraft. Once we are all lined up, the lead elements of this vast assemblage swing on course across the English Channel.

We are now at an altitude of 24,000 feet, where the temperature is a dangerous 50° below zero. Our planes are unpressurized, with wide fuselage openings on both sides where the waist gunners stand ready to swing their 50-caliber machine guns into action. To withstand the extremely cold and rarified air, we are wearing oxygen masks and electrically heated flying suits, boots and gloves. Masks have to be monitored carefully because they sometimes clog up with ice, cutting off a man's oxygen. At this altitude, the exhaust from our engines turns into icy contrails that advertise our presence to the enemy.

As expected, anti-aircraft flak batteries down below open up as we cross the enemy coast. We have good reason to fear flak gunners whose precise rapid firing can put their 88-millimeter shells right at our altitude. Fighter attacks are more dramatic, but steady barrages of massed flak that we must plow through on every mission are devastating.

The first enemy fighters we've ever seen pounce on our group of 26 bombers just before we reach the target. We are leading an element of three planes as our gunners shout "Bandits at 12 o'clock!" Fifty- caliber machine guns begin hammering away, spitting out hundreds of rounds at several Focke Wulf 190's attacking head-on, slicing right through our entire group. I look out the small navigator's window on my left just as a Nazi fighter collides wing-root to wing-root with our wingman. Tangled together in a mass of fiery wreckage, they go down and disappear from view. I turn away from this terrible sight just in time to see our other wingman explode into a huge fireball of flaming fragments with a violent concussion that slams and rocks our plane. This experience sears its way into my memory so vividly that it has come back repeatedly in sudden flashbacks and bad dreams many years later.

As we turn onto the bombing run, flak zeroes in, exploding just ahead of us. The anti-aircraft gunners below are right on target, and we're it. We can see the red-hot centers of the shells as they blow apart, scattering death-dealing chunks of metal and leaving black clouds that look thick enough to walk on. We hear shrapnel tearing through both sides of our fuselage as it echoes and reverberates like a giant aluminum drum. We have no choice but to run the gauntlet right through this frightening barrage because the plane must be held straight and level under bombsight

B-24 Bombers in combat formation.

**Nazi fighter planes, Focke Wulf 190s,
ready to pounce on Allied Bombers.**

**B-24 Bombers flying through flak
as they drop their bombs on target.**

88 mm German Flak guns firing at Allied Bombers.

control so the bombardier can do his job. At long, long last we hear Walt's voice on the intercom shouting "Bombs away!" The plane, relieved of its immense burden, leaps upward. Pete swings us instantly out of the flak inferno to head for home (later we hear a rumor that a flak shell had gone off right under the armored pilot seat of Jimmy Stewart. If true—and it probably was—I never heard him mention it).

Now Pete comes on the intercom. "Anybody hurt?" A chorus of "No's" brings assurance that despite the double onslaught of fighters and flak, nobody aboard has been hit. The plane has also lucked out, with its engines and vulnerable hydraulic systems intact even though the fuselage is riddled with flak fragments. It's hard to believe we're still airborne after the deafening fury of all that shellfire. If all missions are anything like this one, it's hard to imagine how we can survive to finish a mandatory twenty-five-mission tour! My heart keeps pounding until we're safely out to sea with the English coast coming into view, safe from further assaults by fighters.

Once we get back to base, we circle so that other planes with wounded men or severe battle damage can land first. Several planes in distress are firing off smoking red flares to signal emergencies. We keep circling until the planes in trouble have landed before we swing onto the final approach and set our own battered aircraft down safely.

As I leave my position in the plane's nose, I see something has happened that is not uncommon where a man's life is at stake in battle, no matter how brave he is. There's a hunk of yellow ice in the pilot's metal bucket seat. Obviously Pete had a personal problem during the battle. I'm tempted to rib him about wetting his pants under fire, but it isn't something to kid about. Under extreme stress in a "fight or flight" situation, the body evacuates spontaneously. A newspaper columnist and author friend of mine at the Los Angeles Times, Jack Smith, who was a Marine on Guadalcanal, said it happened to him as he hit the beach with Japanese shells bursting and comrades dying all around him. In Pete's case, if his electrically heated body suit had shorted out, he could have suffered serious frostbite.

As we hop down from the plane, we head for the debriefing room. Intelligence officers serve us shots of scotch to relax us before interrogating us about everything we saw and heard during the mission. Crew reports help intelligence officers piece together a comprehensive picture of target results, casualties, and the strength of enemy opposition. By evaluating these reports and reconnaissance photos our commanders will decide what our future mission priorities will be.

Survivors Out On The Town

That evening I ride into the twelfth century town of Norwich in a personnel carrier with other air warriors to go dancing and celebrate surviving. We are combat veterans now, men who know what it feels like to face sudden death at the hands of a determined enemy. As we enter the town's dance hall I spot an apple-cheeked young woman about my age, sitting with several other Norwich maidens waiting for Yanks to ask them to dance. I practically sprint across the floor to make sure I reach Miss Apple Cheeks first. That's how I meet Beryl Fisher. She is warm and gracious, the kind of girl you'd really like to slow-waltz with. We dance to American swing tunes, having a splendid evening, until Beryl's personal curfew time to go home. Not knowing when, if ever, I'll be in town again, I ask if she can return to the dance hall next Saturday night. Beryl agrees, and I walk her almost home. Almost, because she says goodbye on a street corner. "My mum mightn't approve of my dating a Yank," Beryl says. She gives me a friendly peck on the cheek and walks away. By sheer good luck, I manage to have several more evenings between missions with Beryl. We seem to be growing closer and closer, but each date ends the same way, on that same corner. I never push her for an affair or a chance to meet "Mum" because it doesn't feel right to get her emotionally involved with someone flying combat missions.

Relaxing One Day, Terror the Next

Life as an Eighth Air Force flyer feels strangely schizophrenic, with peaceful relaxation and a reasonably normal life on the base one day and the terror of facing death in the sky the next. The only reminders of war in our rural area are the heavy rumblings overhead as a succession of unseen bomber groups assemble in the icy mists above the cloud cover before swinging out over the Channel in a miles-long armada headed for European targets. If it isn't my crew's turn to join the day's raid, I get to spend my time as quietly as I please, lounging around and perhaps enjoying the camaraderie at the day room or the officer's club. Many an evening I catch a ride into town, meet girls and maybe have a romantic dinner date as well. But all too soon I'm grabbing a flak jacket and climbing into a bomber again to gamble my life against battle-hardened enemy fighter squadrons and all that flak that dooms one bomber after another.

Some men, not surprisingly, can't keep coping with the intense mental strain of these crazy-making swings back and forth between life and death. One day, just before boarding our plane for a mission, I notice something strange going on at the flak bin nearby. The bombardier for the plane parked nearest to ours is throwing one flak suit after another into the nose of his bomber. Flak suits are heavy, steel-lined protective jackets to cover your torso front and back, like sandwich boards. As I watch, I realize the bombardier is building a protective nest of flak suits up there in the nose, adding dangerous weight that could force the already heavily loaded plane to crash on takeoff. I know what I have to do.

"Pete!" I yell at my pilot, "I'll be right back!" I run to the flight surgeon standing beside the runway nearby and tell him what's happening. It's obvious the bombardier has suffered all he can take on earlier missions. The flight surgeon immediately grounds the plane and leads the bombardier away as I run back to my ship for takeoff. Needless to say, I feel a deep empathy for that stressed-out airman, who seems to be suffering from combat fatigue. I assume he was taken off flight duty and reassigned, for I never see him around the base again.

Bombing The Buzz Bombers

Our second mission on Christmas Eve, December 24th, 1943, is almost my last. We are sent to attack a factory in Russelsheim making V-1 weapons, those motorized flying "buzz bombs" intended to terrorize Londoners. The V-Is had already had their effect on British civilians, who learned to run for the nearest shelter when the putt-putt of their engines suddenly shuts off overhead. On the way home from Russelsheim I realize that the electric glove on my left hand has shorted out. My fingers are rapidly going numb, being frostbitten by those incredibly cold temperatures at high altitude. If I don't get treatment in time, I could lose those fingers. I call Pete on the intercom and tell him what's happening. He radios ahead to our base that he is coming in with a frostbite victim. The moment we land, an ambulance rushes me to the base hospital where a British doctor is waiting. He is an expert they call in for injuries like mine. They strip me down to the waist and stretch me out on an operating table. Then the doctor inserts a needle deep in my chest near the heart. The injection is a vasodilator to open the blocked capillaries in my hand and restore circulation to the frozen tissue. Three fingers are affected most, the little finger and the two adjoining. They look pale and are totally numb. In the days to follow, the nails darken and I lose two, but the shot is successful

56

in saving the fingers. A few days more, and I'm pronounced fit for duty again.

If our missions have anything in common, it's their unpredictability. One raid threatens to be one of the most dangerous ever attempted. Intelligence has just obtained reconnaissance photos of a high priority secret target near the coast of France. It is a launching site for the V-2, the latest model of Hitler's "Vergeltung's Waffen"—revenge weapons. RAF fighter planes sometimes manage to hunt down the slow-flying V-1's and blow them up before they can cause damage. The new missiles to be launched from our top-secret target are redesigned to fly faster and are thus more dangerous.

What makes our mission so perilous is that we are to go in at a mere 10,000 feet, less than half our normal altitude, to make bombing more accurate. For enemy flak gunners, we'll be like a flock of fat honkers coming in over a duck blind. But what really hammers our morale is when the briefing officer suggests we all write letters home. That's like asking a condemned man if he has any last words. I write my letter, telling mom and dad how much I miss the family, and hoping all is well with them and my twelve-year-old brother. I don't mention the upcoming mission, which probably would be censored out of my V-mail anyhow.

The target is at Bonnieres, France. By the time we reach it I'm hoping for some kind of miracle to spare us from those flak guns. I feel like asking for a blindfold. We might as well be standing up against a wall in front of a firing squad for all the chance we'll have once those 88-millimeter guns open up. *But they don't!* Here we are braced for the worst, expecting a shower of shrapnel at any moment—and not a shot is fired! Wow, what a relief! This is what it must feel like for a man on death row to get a last-moment stay of execution.

Presumably the Germans guarding the launch site held their fire because they didn't want to give away the new weapon's exact location. So what was supposed to be a near-suicidal mission ended up being a milk run. It turned out to be *the only mission* we ever flew when our aircraft was not hit by flak or fighters—or both.

CHAPTER NINE

A DESPERATE GAMBLE

Today it's cold and heavily overcast with a biting wind blowing over the snowy ground. I'm bundled up in a fleece-lined flight jacket, boots and gloves, headed for the mess hall for lunch. Our crew isn't flying today or tomorrow, so I'm grateful for a little free time. As I walk into the mess hall, I spot our bombardier, Walt at a corner table, all by himself. I've been worried about him lately. He looks exhausted, as if he hasn't slept well for days. Being a bombardier and manning twin fifty-caliber machine guns in the nose of the plane is like having a seat on the front line when enemy fighters make a head-on attack. Obviously the stress of combat and seeing so many other bombers going down in flames is taking its toll on Walt. All of us are feeling it. He barely glances up as I set my tray down across from him.

"How's it going?" I ask. He gestures wearily, as if there is nothing to say. We sit there in silence for a while, eating our spam, mashed potatoes and gravy. Then he looks up at me with those dark circles etched under his eyes and says, "I'm flying a mission with another crew tomorrow." This is stunning news. Why would he want to put his life on the line with another crew at a time like this? When I ask him, he hesitates and then says, "They needed a guy."

"C'mon, Walt. You're our bombardier and we have a great crew. Did you discuss this with Pete?"

He shakes his head.

"They ask and you do it? Just like that?"

The answer comes slowly.

"I wanted to. It was my idea."

"But why, Walt? Why?"

"Because I want to get my 25 missions over with and go home. I just want to *go home*." He sinks back into his chair and looks away.

Well, who can blame him? We all want to finish our missions and wake up from this nightmare of aerial slaughter. But I'm convinced that if Walt wants to see home and family again, volunteering for extra missions at the height of the air war is exactly the wrong thing to do.

"Walt, we all want to go home, but this isn't a very good time to be volunteering."

"What's the difference?"

"The Germans are still throwing everything they have at us, and casualties are high on both sides. But they can't keep it up much longer. We're getting more and more P-51 fighter escorts while the Germans just have to be running out of planes and pilots. Our best shot is to hang in there, fly the missions we're told to fly, and try to outlast the Luftwaffe." Walt thought a moment, and then said, "Maybe you're right, Ray—but I gave my word. I'm flying tomorrow." His mind is made up. I reach across the table and offer my hand. "Good luck out there, Walt."

Next afternoon on January 5th, 1944, the plane with Walt aboard bombs the heavily fortified port of Kiel on the north coast of Germany. Witnesses report the plane goes down under heavy attack over the target. Parachutes are seen of surviving crewmen, but word soon comes that Walt didn't make it. Like so many thousands of 8th Air Force crewmen, he will never come home again. All of us on our crew are terribly saddened by Walt's loss. We can't help wondering…who will be next?

CHAPTER TEN
JUST HOPING
TO SURVIVE

As our group flies more and more missions, an ominous trend begins to emerge. Judging by our casualties, it doesn't seem likely that the average crewmember will survive the mandatory tour of 25 missions and be rotated home. The Eighth Air Force is mounting unprecedented thousand-plane raids over Germany. A desperately determined Luftwaffe is fighting back with everything it has, suffering as well as inflicting high casualties. I say nothing about my gloomy thoughts to my crew buddies, but I can't help wondering how many of us will last long enough to see our loved ones again. How many more war department telegrams will inform families that their airmen sons have been killed in action? Or that they are in enemy hands, behind barbed wire in prison camps? All we have to go on is what's been happening to our own comrades in the four squadrons of the 445th Bomb Group. There are times when every plane we send out on a mission returns. But sometimes planes that make it back are shot up so badly that they carry dead and wounded. Still others stagger in so heavily damaged that they crash on landing, breaking apart or catching fire. Worst of all are those terrible days when several of our group's bombers don't come back at all.

Flying a series of bomber runs on Germany is considered by military experts to be one of the most dangerous and physically demanding tasks of the entire air war. Sortie rates are high because of pressure to win an early aerial victory, and long-range fighter escorts just aren't available for the earliest missions. About one-fourth of returning bombers sustain some kind of damage. The normal maximum tour of 25 missions in a heavy bomber—the most dangerous of all—leaves a crew member with less than a 50% chance of escaping death or physical harm. Only one-fourth of crewmembers can expect to complete their tours![4] But at last the Eighth Air Force is steadily building up enough crews, planes and munitions to keep mounting massive, thousand bomber assaults while the hard-pressed Luftwaffe is running out of pilots. Clearly the Allies intend to drive the Luftwaffe from its own skies in time for the invasion of Europe, expected this summer. Air supremacy over the beaches might well make the difference between a successful and a failed invasion. I figure our best chance as airmen is to survive long enough to see the odds come down, as they eventually must.

My crew takes pride in never missing a mission assignment. We never abort unless radioed by division headquarters to turn back because of bad weather developing over the target or back at base. But lately we're hearing whispered rumors that some individual crews have aborted on high-risk missions, reporting more mechanical problems than average. I'm skeptical about such rumors. Missions ordered are carried out, period. On the other hand, I wouldn't know whether the rumors are true of individual crews. I do know morale is suffering as more and more bunks lie empty, and ground personnel come around to collect the footlockers and other personal effects of those who are missing in action.

A "Harmless" Prank

The Eighth Air Force and the RAF, already pounding Germany into rubble with round-the clock bombing, intensify their efforts even further during the opening months of 1944. The Luftwaffe is stretched near its limits, but it still has plenty of fight left on February 13th when our crew is sent on what turns out to be our ninth and roughest mission yet. The first time we bombed a buzz bomb site in France had been a milk run. Not this one. Our orders are to drop our bombs when the flight leader does, so I follow an impulse to play a harmless prank on the new bombardier, Lt. John J. Heany. While he's locked in the nose turret, I'll drop the bombs myself! Releasing our bomb load when the lead bombardier drops his doesn't require a bombsight. All I have to do is push a lever behind and below the nose turret. But just as I'm crouching down, letting the bombs go, a flak shell slams through the nose plexiglas beneath the bombardier's turret and passes directly over my head. It explodes right where I would usually be standing at the navigator's desk. It blows my radio to bits, pins my map to the desk with fragments, and sends a big hunk of shrapnel flying on up between the co-pilot's rudder pedals, hitting Tom right in the stomach. The radioman and crew chief come to his aid, trying to stanch the wound with bandages and compresses. By some near-miracle, no fragments find me. Meanwhile more flak shells are slashing into the fuselage, creating major damage.

Pete swings the plane around out of the flak for home and comes on the intercom to alert us to our worsening situation: "Tom's been hit pretty bad, and we're losing altitude. If we try to get him back to a hospital, I'm not sure if we can make it over the cliffs of Dover. If we ditch in the English Channel instead, Search and Rescue could pick us up—but that might be too late for Tom. So let's vote. All those in favor of trying to reach a hospital on the English coast, say 'aye.'" "Aye!" comes an instant chorus over the intercom. We are still losing altitude with every passing minute as we reach the French Coast and head out over the channel. Maybe we'll clear the cliffs and maybe we won't. Pete orders everything possible thrown out the waist windows to lighten the load. Out go machine guns, flak suits and heavy ammo boxes. Soon nothing is left but our parachutes. Now the cliffs are looming up, closer and closer. We barely manage to skim over them, and Pete sets us down almost immediately in a bumpy landing at the nearest airfield.

An ambulance races up to our battered bomber. A medic jumps out, sticks his head into the nose compartment and asks, "Where's the navigator?"

"I'm the navigator," I answer.

He looks surprised. "Then who's hurt?"

"Our co-pilot."

I can see why the medic is confused. The most visible damage to our plane is up front at the navigator's station where that shell exploded. The medics load Tom on a gurney, do what they can to stabilize him, and speed away to the base hospital. The rest of us board a truck taking us back to our home base at Tibenham. The surgeons do their best, but late that night we get the news we feared the most: Tom didn't make it. A few days later, on a dismal, drizzly afternoon, we survivors of his crew gather at the graveside in the new American cemetery at Cambridge as our beloved buddy is buried with full military honors. An honor guard in full dress uniform fires volleys in salute. A bugler plays taps. I keep thinking that Tom might still be alive today—and I'd probably be dead—if he hadn't been struck by a shell that so narrowly missed me. The Tom we all mourn on this saddest of days was such a decent, thoughtful and kindly young man. He would have made a good husband and father, like so many other men on both sides in this terrible war. I feel the tears on my cheeks. I shall be grieving for Tom for the rest of my life.

CHAPTER ELEVEN
BAD WEATHER, BAD NEWS

A thick blanket of overcast settles in over Britain and Western Europe for the next several days, forcing a lull in bombing raids. It's more dangerous to fly and almost impossible to hit targets with any likelihood of success whenever bad weather blots them out. But these clouds bring precious days of rest for battle-weary aircrews like ours that can use a respite from combat. I'm down with a bad head cold, so I'm not fit for duty anyhow. My ear tubes are plugged up—one of the worst things that can happen to a flyer in an unpressurized plane. If our ears stuff up and can't "pop" to equalize inner and outer pressure, the pain can be excruciating and we risk permanent hearing damage. I am truly miserable with what feels like the mother of all colds when I go on sick call at the base dispensary. I'm weak and dizzy, sinuses pounding with a brutal headache. The flight surgeon peers up my nose and down my throat, and orders me taken off the duty rosters. He treats my sinuses by poking long medicated swabs way up both nostrils. With those swabs sticking out I look like a walrus. After several minutes the flight surgeon removes the swabs, the sinuses unplug and I feel almost instant relief. This method of treatment is dramatically effective, the medical version of a plumber's roto-rooter. Then a nurse puts me to bed in the hospital ward to be monitored until my ears clear completely.

Meanwhile, the weather is improving somewhat, with mostly cloudy skies moving in to replace the heavy cloud cover that's been blocking the sun. The next morning, February 24, 1944, I awake to the massive droning overhead of bomber engines as our group forms up for another mission. Where are they heading? Is my crew up there with another navigator? I hope not. We've tempted fate enough lately on rough missions against fierce opposition. Late this afternoon I hear the heavy rumbling overhead again as our bombers return to base. Sometime later the nurse comes to my bed. I take one look at her and think uh-oh, here comes bad news. She puts a comforting hand on my shoulder and says softly, "I'm very sorry to tell you this, Lieutenant. Your crew was shot down on the Gotha raid over Germany today." "Oh, no!" I'd been thinking it had to happen sooner or later, as it had to so many other crews in our Group. "Did anybody see parachutes?" She nods and brightens a bit. "They saw several chutes pop open. There's a good chance your crew survived."

"Thank God for that!" If I hadn't caught a heavy cold, I'd probably have been out there in one of those chutes, on my way to a German prison camp. "Doctor says you'll be leaving us tomorrow." I nod. My ear passages have cleared up and I'm ready to leave the hospital. But I'm not ready to fly. Not yet. I'm an emotional mess. *I've lost my crew!* How am I going to face finishing a tour of 25 missions without those guys? I have to do it. That's what I'm here for. But I'm so depressed I can hardly think about it.

Lost in Grief

Next morning I check out of sick bay and report to headquarters. A young Group Administration Captain, one of the officers we call "ground grippers" because they don't fly, sits me down in his office and sympathizes with my loss in a soft and kindly way. I'm thinking he's done a lot of this lately. I just sit there listening, or trying to. My mind keeps tuning in and out until he says something that really catches my attention. He says that because of my loss, I am being granted two weeks compassionate leave. Two weeks! Oh, man! I feel a tremendous surge of gratitude and relief. I know I can use every second of that time to pull myself back together before returning to combat.

Now the Captain tells me what he knows about my crew's last flight. He says it was by far the costliest the 445th has flown yet. Of the twenty-five planes that went out, only twelve came back. The group was under relentless and unremitting assault by both fighters and flak *for more than two hours*, far longer than the usual hit-and-run fighter attacks which are bad enough, bringing death and destruction with lightning swiftness. Witnesses reported that Pete's crew fought to the last, knocking two enemy fighters out of the sky before their own plane was shot to pieces and the crew had to bail out. The mission overall was a success in that the bombs landed right on target, earning our group a high honor, the Presidential Unit Citation. But the cost was very high: 52% casualties and the loss of 130 airmen *in just one afternoon*.

Hal Turell, a lead navigator with my own 703rd Squadron, was on that mission. Thanks to his remarkably detailed combat diary, I found out what happened to the 445th that day in the skies over Gotha. His diary brings to life the ferocity and chaos of aerial combat:

"We are briefed to attack the Gothaer Wagon Werks, an aircraft factory that produces the Messerschmitt Me-110. It will be a deep penetration of enemy territory and we all have had very bad premonitions about this mission. The attrition rate on experienced crews has been quite heavy. Our chances of surviving to complete a tour are now one in three. To gain extra crews, the 8th Air Force has extended the mission tour from 25 to 30 and told us to fly with a nine-man crew. This means leaving one gunner behind. Because all of us are quite apprehensive about this mission, we load the ship with extra ammunition so that it barely can take off. After all, each gun can fire one thousand rounds of ammunition in two minutes.

"Europe is clear, cold and covered with snow, ideal for a daylight raid. The Germans know that too and are ready for us. Thirty crews climb into their B-24 Liberators and take off. By the time we head out over the North Sea, five planes have turned back because of various malfunctions. The remaining twenty-five press on. We are fifteen minutes ahead of schedule at this point. We missed our rendezvous with our fighter cover. This will cost us dearly in the hours ahead.

"Sergeant Billy McClellan is flying in the ball turret this day. As the formation crosses the North Sea he can see enemy fighters picking off some B-17s that had aborted their formation and turned back to England. Mac sees eight of these Flying Fortresses go down into the icy waters. No parachutes could save them from the freezing depths. A man would live just two minutes at those temperatures. Our group leader keeps calling for the high fighter cover to come down. They do. They are Germans!

"First they come in waves of fighters, line abreast, then form a queue and come roaring in one after the other. Other fighters stand off at a distance and fire rockets into the formation. Dive-bombers come through with a large ball hanging on the end of a cable about 100 feet long. We hear the tail gunner, Sergeant Bill Adair, say some enemy fighters, after their frontal pass, are blowing up after they are a mile or so past the group. It looks as though three or four hundred fighters are working over our Combat Wing with special emphasis on our group. Mac is overjoyed to see two German fighters collide on two occasions, they are so thick.

"Our lead plane is hit and does a slow roll towards us. At the same time, about five German fighters come right at us as we are now outside the formation. Our pilot, Lieutenant Ralph Stimmel, is able to sideslip our plane when the frontal pass comes. This throws their aim off considerably. One of our lead ships catches a direct hit. It explodes, sending airplane and body parts through the formation and doing considerable damage to other ships.

"One ME-109 comes head on into one of our group and blows off a Liberator's nose. As the ship goes spinning down, the 109 pulls up into a steep climb. The top turret gunner of the following B-24 puts a long burst into him. The 109 falls off on its back and goes down through the formation, crashing into another Liberator in the low element and taking off its whole tail section. This ship heads up into the bomb bay of another Lib and the two planes collide. One goes sailing through the formation, scattering it. Breaking a formation is the German fighter pilot's dream. The 445th fortunately has their most experienced crews out this day and the formation quickly recovers, with each ship taking its place as though it's a drill every time an incident like this occurs.

"On the bomb run, another fighter comes within 100 yards of the lead plane and releases a parachute bomb that the B-24 runs head on into. The explosion tears the entire top section of the plane off back to the wing. It then catches fire and slides tail first to the ground. The deputy lead takes over and continues the bomb run. Then the plane on our right wing gets hit and goes into a loop, heading right for us. Ralph has some frantic jockeying to clear him and get back in formation.

"The attacks continue through the approach, the bomb run, and for another hour and a half after bombs away. We lose seven planes before the bombing and six more afterwards, thirteen out of twenty-five. We do reach and accurately bomb the target and shoot down twenty-three German fighters. Ironically the fighter attacks have driven us down to 15,000 feet, which substantially helps our bombing accuracy. We are fortunate that the group had a large complement of experienced crews flying this day. Because of that, we reach the target and many survive.

"The action was fast, furious and enveloped in the fog of battle. At one point someone in a parachute comes floating through our formation. He is close enough that I can see that he is unconscious. He seems to be an American and is lightly dressed in green fatigues, which is surprising. (I still wonder if he was alive and if he survived.) Another crewman bails out and opens his chute too soon. The tail of one of the low element bombers catches it and his parachute is shredded. One more enemy fighter comes in close and shoots off the tail of another Lib. As the fighter turns, the Lib's gunners get him and he bails out. At the same time two men from the stricken plane parachute out and the three descend together with much arm waving and gestures.

"At one point our wingman has his top turret shot off with so much damage that we wonder what is keeping him up. We can see the copilot wiping the blood away with one hand while he flies the ship with the other. We lose him later. As he slides off to oblivion, I say to Ralph we better get out of here or we will all be dead. Ralph still has his sense of humor and dryly says, 'Where would you suggest we go?' I scan the horizon and there are no other formations to be seen.

"Of the 12 surviving planes, only 8 return to the base. The others have so much battle damage they have to land at alternative bases. One of the many ironies of war is that the position we flew that day was high outside. The two most dangerous and exposed airplanes in a formation are high outside and low outside, commonly called 'coffin corners.' Both planes flying this most dreaded position survived! On the way back, two P-38's, each with an engine out, join us for mutual protection. When we get to the Channel they wave us farewell.

"Ours was the only crew of our squadron to return to our Tibenham base. The ship we were flying was incredibly shot up, yet we suffered no wounds. At the debriefing everyone was appalled and wanted to know what happened. There were a number of reporters there as well. We were still in shock and in disbelief that we had lived. Our squadron commander, Jimmy Stewart, listened intently to us. We were the first crew into the debriefing room. He asked us details and then tears came to his eyes and he left the room for a little while.

"There was a young American Red Cross girl there with candy for us. As the story of that day penetrated to her, she put her hand to her mouth and ran away. We cleaned out the candy. The bombing was the most accurate we ever did and destroyed the target. We also flew with a ten-man crew after that."

Bad as the losses were, our 445th Bomb Group suffered even higher losses on September 27, 1944 when it put 35 B-24 Liberators into the air to join more than a thousand other bombers to target Kassel, an important transportation and communications area in central Germany. Our group somehow got slightly off course while all the others went on to the target. After dropping its bombs, our group turned for home, all alone and terribly vulnerable to attack. German fighters—150 of them!—saw their opportunity, came in behind them and attacked so savagely that within three minutes 25 bombers were shot down, and 29 fighters destroyed! Of the 10 bombers that survived this incredible onslaught, only four made it back to base. Two others made emergency landings at another base in Manston, England. One of the latter was piloted by Lt. Bill Dewey, whose plane had a 3-foot hole in it and several wounded crewmen. Dewey subsequently founded the Kassel Mission Memorial Association as a Veterans organization to honor the 118 men of the 445th Group who lost their lives that day, as well as the survivors. "It was the largest loss by any bomb group in any single day in any single battle in history. It should be in the history books right there next to Custer's Last Stand," says the late Lt. Dewey's daughter, Linda Alice Dewey of Glen Arbor, MI, now President of the Kassel Mission Historical Society.

CHAPTER TWELVE

A BREAK FROM COMBAT

I'm very grateful for a two-week break from combat. I keep seeing the faces of my buddies who didn't come back. I keep fighting tears. My nerves are shot. Yet I need to get through this somehow to fly a dozen more missions and finish my tour of duty. As for choosing how to spend my leave, I decide to go to London. I know that everything worth doing as a tourist can be done in that historic city, the very heart of Britain. As my train from Norwich arrives in London, on this cold February day in 1944, I see evidence of war everywhere: protective barrage balloons anchored on cables, bombed-out flats, rubble-strewn shops and huge craters left by direct hits during 58 straight days of German bombing attacks back in September 1940. An aerial armada of 348 Luftwaffe bombers escorted by 617 fighters set off fires that burned out of control and spread everywhere. Hundreds of civilian flats and industrial area buildings were set ablaze. Every morning families of Londoners emerged from bomb shelters to see new scenes of devastation.

Hitler's Fatal Mistake

Germany was fully prepared to invade and defeat Britain with 260,000

The bombing of London during World War II.

Firemen work to stop the fires in London
after an air attack by the Germans.

troops as soon as it knocked the Royal Air Force out of action. This plan might have brought the Nazis an early victory if attacks on the RAF had continued. There was only one British Division at home to oppose an invasion, plus the Home Guard, consisting of old men with nothing to fight with but personal weapons and outdated armory guns.

In the spring of 1940, the Germans launched their assault on the vastly outnumbered RAF and all its airfields as the necessary prelude to invasion. The RAF men, flying 1,000 sorties—separate flights—a day, were so exhausted that they fell asleep as soon as they landed and pulled off the runway. In just two weeks, German planes succeeded in shooting down a quarter of the RAF's 900 pilots! Britain couldn't sustain such losses much longer. But then something totally unexpected happened. Adolph Hitler, embarrassed and enraged that the RAF has bombed Berlin, ordered the mighty Luftwaffe to switch from RAF bases to a vengeful, all-out assault on London. He wanted to see RAF fighters going down over their own capitol. But this switch in strategy was a major blunder. It took the pressure off the RAF, whose pilots lived to fight another day. By September, as weather worsened, Hitler had no choice but to cancel the invasion. The heavy assault on London continued unmercifully until the following May, when Hitler finally shifted his bombers eastward to prepare for the invasion of Soviet Russia.

Britain's Prime Minister, Winston Churchill, paid the RAF pilots a memorable tribute to their gallantry:

"The gratitude of every home in our Island, in our Empire, and indeed throughout the world, except in the abodes of the guilty, goes out to the British airmen who, undaunted by odds, unwearied in their constant challenge and mortal danger, are turning the tide of the world war by their prowess and by their devotion. Never in the field of human conflict was so much owed by so many to so few."

A Ray Of Sunshine

At the London train station, I take a cab to a modest hotel. I'm not feeling up for doing anything on this cold, cloudy and cheerless day, so I settle for a meandering walk in a nearby park. As I approach a bench where an elderly Brit is all bundled up in a heavy overcoat, a solitary shaft of sunlight breaks through the cloud cover and shines directly on the old gentleman, like a spotlight from heaven. He glances upward in surprised delight and then smiles at me, saying, "What a lovely afternoon!"

Next morning I awake thinking I'd better get my act together. I can't sit around grieving all day, no matter how bad I feel. I remind myself that this break from combat is a fleeting chance to see one of the greatest cities in all history, founded by the Romans two thousand years ago. I get out some maps and spend the next several days riding the underground tube to places that tourists flock to see from all over the world. My first choice is St. Paul's Cathedral, built three centuries ago by the famed architect, Sir Christopher Wren. I can't help admiring its magnificent mosaics, said to be the result of Queen Victoria's complaint that the church interior was "most dreary, dingy and undevotional." I also go to see Westminster Abbey, the medieval cathedral where Britain's royalty has been crowned ever since William the Conqueror took the throne nearly ten centuries ago on Christmas Day, 1066.

Wherever I go in my U.S. Army Air Corps uniform with its silver wings, the Brits greet me warmly. Bone-weary of war, they are counting on us Yanks to turn the tide and help bring victory to their long and immensely brave struggle against the Nazis. There's plenty to see and do here, but I also dearly wish to see Scotland's Edinburgh while I have the chance. It means a four-hour ride on British railways, a pleasure in itself. I travel in a compartment with an elderly English couple that cautions me, delicately but earnestly, that the Scots are "a different kind of people." Not unfriendly, mind you, but ah, different. The Scots I'm soon to meet offer the same advice about the English. It reminds me of the rivalry back home between Los Angeles and San Francisco.

Snow is falling in large wet flakes that blur the railway carriage windows as we arrive in Edinburgh, rightly regarded as one of the most beautiful cities anywhere. I take shelter in a nearby tea shoppe, sipping their famous tea and nibbling away at tasty scones. When I come out, I'm surprised by three old ladies who think it's great fun to toss snowballs at a Yank. They are laughing and whooping, having a rather merry old time as they barrage me with snowballs. I'm laughing too hard to fling any back at them. One of these ladies has an arm like a series pitcher, winding up before she scores several direct hits, splattering snow all over me. It's great fun and lifts my spirits. I spend the next few remaining days of my leave wandering all over town through crunchy snowdrifts. I trudge up the royal mile of Princes Street to the old castle that sits on a high crag. This was the home in medieval times of Scotland's kings and queens. The view is panoramic. I can see from this spectacular vantage point why the Scots are so proud of their beautiful capitol. The trip has been something of a tonic after all, and that's a good thing, because I report back for duty tomorrow.

CHAPTER THIRTEEN

DOWN IN FLAMES

As I board the southbound train to return to duty my mood saddens again. I have this edgy, ominous feeling that my luck is running out. Is it a premonition? It's probably just a recognition that the odds are against my finishing a tour of duty. Can I survive another dozen missions? Not likely. I try to shake off these forebodings. I'll need my wits about me to deal with whatever fate now awaits me in that insane lottery of lives in the skies over Europe. Up there, four miles above the earth, bullets and shells don't have names on them. They are "To Whom It May Concern." They strike at random, and you die at random. If you're lucky, you return from your mission. If you're in the wrong place at the wrong time, like Walt and Tom and the rest of my crew, you don't come back.

When I report to our base at Tibenham I am immediately assigned to a replacement crew led by pilot Robert B. Parker, no relation, from Mahoning County, Ohio. I've never met him before and know nothing about him, but then he doesn't know me either. He welcomes me to the crew with a warm handshake, which I appreciate.

This time the fateful red string on the intelligence map stretches farther than ever across Germany. It reaches all the way to Friedrichshafen, on the shores of Lake Constance near the Swiss border. We had heard that some American fliers were already interned in neutral Switzerland,

and their lives were said to be quite pleasant. So, if we had our choice, this would be the best mission to get shot down on. All is going well as we cross the French coast and head inland toward Germany, but after about 15 minutes Robert swings us out of combat formation and turns around to abort the mission. He comes on the intercom and says, "We've lost an engine and can't keep up, so we're turning back." All of us know that's bad news, because bombers that have to leave formation are sitting ducks. Fighters have all the advantages of speed and maneuverability. But we haven't seen any fighters yet, so maybe we can reach the coast before they can pick us up and shoot us down. If our luck holds out, we may actually make it back to England. The pilot starts a gradual descent in the area of Rouen. We take off our oxygen masks when we reach 10,000 feet. So far, so good.

Then it happens! Two Focke-Wulf 190's come diving down out of the sun and riddle the plane with machine gun bullets, setting it afire. Both Robert and co-pilot Lt. Richard J. Pear of Indiana are killed instantly, and our doomed plane drifts off into a flat spin. Flight Engineer T/Sgt. Joseph E. McDonnell of Bexar County, Texas and Gunner Staff Sgt. Wallace C. Luce of Ashtabula County, Ohio have also been killed. Smoke is rapidly filling the nose compartment. I react instinctively, crawling to the forward escape hatch with my chest chute strapped on. I open the hatch to bail out, but then realize that I'd better check before jumping to see if the bombardier is trapped in the nose turret. The centrifugal force of the spin is increasing as I struggle to back away from the hatch. It's becoming almost impossible to move. I'm unaware that the bombardier is already out of his turret and has come up behind me with flames licking at his flight coveralls and burning his neck. Seeing me hunched over the hatch, he thinks I'm dead—so he puts his boot on the back of my head and pushes me out!

That's how I find myself outside the plane, tumbling head over heels and dropping faster and faster toward earth in a free fall. I don't dare pull the ripcord because I haven't fastened the leg straps yet that absorb the sudden shock when the chute pops open. The straps are flapping wildly as I tumble downward while trying in vain to grab them. Since I have no idea how close I am to hitting the ground, I give up trying to catch the straps. Instead I grab the chute webbing on my chest with both hands in a vise-like grip, pin my elbows tightly against my sides to brace against the coming shock, and pull the ripcord as my feet are pointing earthward. I'm gambling that I can hang on when that chute opens, and not be hurled out into space. I'd never heard of anybody trying a stunt like this and living to tell about it. But suddenly, as the opening chute yanks me up and away, I realize that this most desperate of ideas is actually working! I come down clinging white-knuckled to those webbing straps, not daring to reach upward for the shroud lines to guide my descent for fear I'll slip out.

I look down at the earth, still thousands of feet below, feeling immense relief just to be alive. It's actually quite pleasant to be drifting quietly downward on this beautiful sunny spring day, March 18th, 1944, listening to the gentle flap-flap of the parachute. As I twist around in my chute to look back the way we came, I see the bombardier's chute about half a mile away. He's dropping at a faster rate because he's a big, solid man who weighs at least fifty pounds more than I do. I think of the others aboard. Did any survive? Three crewmen who bailed out were captured. They were Cpl. Joe C. Watson of Kern County, California, the radio operator; S/Sgt. James P. Cass of New York City, the assistant engineer, and S/Sgt. Kenneth F. Bradford, a gunner from North Carolina. A gunner from my original crew who also missed its last flight, Sgt. Ned A. Daugherty, jumped at the last possible moment. His chute swung only once before he landed, so the Germans didn't see him and he managed to escape back to England with the help of the French Underground.

After a descent that seems to last forever, I hit the ground in a plowed field, barely missing a fence, and spraining my ankle so badly I can't walk.

So Where's the French Underground?

I remember what our intelligence officers taught us to do in a situation like this—bury the chute and the yellow "Mae West" life preserver to leave no clues where I've landed. I do this on my hands and knees, clawing the soft earth with both hands as fast as I can. Then I look around for a place to hide until sundown. I see a farmhouse about a quarter mile away and a heavily wooded area at the farm's edge, just a couple of hundred feet from me. Fine. I'll head for the woods before any Germans show up. Then I can sneak out to the farmhouse after dark. With any luck I'll find a sympathizer there to put me in touch with the French Underground. I wouldn't be the first flier to elude capture and get back to England with their help. I set out for the trees, hopping fast as I can on my right foot to keep weight off my rapidly swelling left ankle. Once inside the tree line, I lie down and cover myself up with spring leaves, figuring they'll blend in

B-24 hit by enemy fire.

A hard landing in a parachute.

with my green coveralls for camouflage.

Great scheme, huh? Okay, so it was obvious. But there are two rather relevant facts that I'm about to learn the hard way. One is that there's a large contingent of German infantry bivouacked (camped) in these woods, poised to move against the Allied invasion they are expecting. They have seen our chutes pop open and followed them down with their field glasses, so they know almost exactly where the bombardier and I have come to earth. The other awkward fact is that I'm not aware that part of my coveralls has been burned away, exposing the bright blue heated underwear underneath!

As I lie there motionless, eyes closed, I hear footsteps approaching. Uh-oh. A search party. I hear an approaching soldier saying they've found one of those goddamned terror flyers and the other one has to be right around here. Gulp! Now those three years I spent studying German in high school might come in handy. The footsteps come closer, closer—and then stop. I'm not even breathing, holding absolutely still. Then a voice directly above me says, "Allo!" The game is up. They got me! I open my eyes and find I'm staring into the barrel of a rifle, just inches away, held by a German Private. Beside him stands his portly Sergeant, smiling like a hunter who has run his prey to earth.

"Steh auf!" commands the Private, gesturing with his gun.

I get up, balancing on one leg.

"Haende hoch!" I raise my hands.

"Wo ist deine Pistole?"

"Ich habe keine Pistole." I'm saying I don't have a gun. He can scarcely believe it. I left it behind in the burning plane.

"Keine Pistole?"

"Keine."

Without warning he swings a roundhouse right that catches me on the side of the jaw and knocks me down.

"Nein, nein!" the Sergeant protests. "Er ist ein kriegsgefangener!" He's telling the private that he can't hit me because I'm a prisoner of war. I rub my jaw, appreciating the Sergeant's thought, if not the timing. Now they pull me to my feet, and the Private grudgingly assists me in walking to their nearby encampment. As they sit me down at an outdoor table for questioning, the Sergeant says, "Fuer Sie ist der Krieg vorbei." It's a simple statement that says so much: *For you, the war is over.* The way the Sergeant says it makes me think he envies me. I was to hear these same words again and again from Germans who'd had a bellyful of war, and probably of Hitler as well.

Wait a Minute! He's Speaking German?

The Sergeant begins asking routine questions. Then it suddenly seems to dawn on both soldiers that I've been answering in their own language. The Sergeant asks "Wo haben Sie Deutsch gelernt?" I tell him I learned German in high school, that my mother speaks German and her parents were born in Germany.

Mom's father, Max Frick, left Germany for America well before World War I to avoid being conscripted into the Army. I doubt it's a good idea to share that ironic fact with my questioner. The Sergeant would probably much rather be sipping a good German lager in Milwaukee right now, if he had the choice, instead of waiting here to fight the mighty armada that will surely land thousands of Allied troops on the French beaches in the near future. The Sergeant looks off, having his own thoughts. Then he turns back to me with a frown and asks the big question: "Warum kaempfen Sie gegen Deutschland?" His question is deceptive in its simplicity. *Why are you fighting against Germany?*

What can I say? That my grandfather came to America for its freedoms and I was defending them? The Sergeant might have accepted a relatively mild answer like that, but I am a frightened young man in the hands of the enemy. I fear that any honest answer might get me into more trouble than I am already. So instead I imagine myself in the Sergeant's combat boots and come up with the kind of answer that might make sense to a soldier in Hitler's Amy:

"Roosevelt hat es mir befohlen!" *Roosevelt made me do it!*

"Ach, ja!" says the Sergeant. Both he and the Private nod with what seems to be heartfelt understanding. Whatever German soldiers are doing these latter days as victory and morale slip away, Hitler is making them do it.

CHAPTER FOURTEEN
A GERMAN SOLDIER
OF HONOR

There are marvelous places all over France to enjoy gourmet dining, but the Rouen City Jail was never among them. I have my first dinner as a prisoner of war there after my captors bring me to town and dump me off. There is no menu and only one entrée—horsemeat. It isn't bad when sauced with hunger. It's also an unforgettable meal, because I won't eat that well again until the war is over.

The next morning, guards escort me to a small prisoner facility in nearby Beauvais. I'll be there for two weeks until the Germans collect enough of us downed airmen to be sent on via Paris to a permanent POW camp in northern Germany. All of us are unkempt, unshaven and in dire need of a shower. We're wearing the same flying outfits we had on when we got shot down. After several days more in a Paris jail we are herded aboard a charcoal-burning, smoke-belching, hiccupping German Army truck that takes us to the rail station. I wonder what the driver would think if he knew we were the guys who bombed Germany's refineries and deprived him of a truck with real gasoline.

A night train bound for Germany is waiting to take us to the notorious Dulag Luft Interrogation Center in Oberusel, outside of Frankfurt. No Allied flyers are ever sent on to a permanent POW camp until German Intelligence specialists grill them at Dulag Luft for every scrap of information of any use in the air war.

At the train depot, our captors divide us into small groups to be escorted by soldiers going home on furlough. That's how I meet Sergeant Schmidt, as I'll call him because I never learned his real name. He is a decent and intelligent man in his early fifties. I remember him vividly to this day with respect and gratitude. He and I sit up for hours on the night train to Frankfurt, talking in German as best I can about how World War I led to World War II. The Sergeant brings up Wilson's 14 Points, which America's President Woodrow Wilson had proposed in 1918 as a fair peace settlement. But instead the victors saddled a defeated Germany with huge reparation payments that caused bitter and lasting resentments. Adolph Hitler, leader of the new Nazi Party, rose to dictatorial power as Fuhrer in large part by fanning the flames of those resentments. He built a resurgent Germany with an incredibly powerful and seemingly unstoppable modern military machine, and led the German people into World War II.

Despite my limited vocabulary, the Sergeant and I manage to understand each other. He impresses me as a thoughtful, kind, and melancholy man. The melancholy surfaces when he tells me his wife died in a bombing raid. There is nothing I can say to his overwhelming loss except to express the deepest sympathy of one human being for another.

Another Brush With Death

Next morning we hear the air raid sirens wailing as the train is pulling into Darmstadt, a railhead not far from Frankfurt. The Sergeant leaps to his feet and tells me, "Es gibt Luftangriff! Wir muessen aussteigen und in einen Luftschutzkeller gehen! Mach schnell!" It's an air raid! We've got to get off and go to an air protection cellar. Hurry ! I tell the other prisoners "They're taking us to a shelter. Let's go!" As we jump down onto the station platform, four prisoners and four guards, a woman's voice over the loudspeakers warns what's happening: "Achtung, Achtung! Feindliche bomber kommen!" Attention, attention! Enemy bombers are coming! The Sergeant and his men hurry us down the stairs into an underground shelter where the German passengers, mostly women and children are also heading. We find seats on benches below as a teen-aged soldier, far too young to be in uniform, keeps his rifle pointed right at us. Soon we hear ground-shaking explosions coming closer and closer, louder and louder, rocking the shelter like a major earthquake. "Christ, they're hitting close!" says one of my comrades. So this is what feels like to be down here under our bombs. It's very scary. No wonder the Germans call us "terror flyers." The civilians huddling together on the benches around us cringe as each stick of bombs detonates above, and so do we.

When the raid finally ends, the guards take us back upstairs to the rail platform. We're not surprised to see that our train is "kaput"—destroyed. Repair crews are already clearing away twisted rails, but it will probably be hours before any more trains can get through. Sgt. Schmidt tells me he'll have to take us to nearby Frankfurt by bus. As our bus pulls into a main square in Frankfurt, buildings are ablaze and collapsing in ruins all around us. Pick and shovel crews are pushing dump carts along the streets as they clear away huge heaps of rubble. Tensions rise suddenly as the workers catch sight of us getting off the bus in our flight suits. They shake their fists at us, as if they think we've just been shot down in the raid and are responsible for all this flaming destruction. Several laborers abandon their carts and start coming toward us, brandishing those picks and shovels like a lynch mob. Sgt. Schmidt immediately realizes their murderous intent. He tells me in German, "Tell your men to form a tight circle and look down at the ground. We will protect you," Obviously he doesn't want us to be seen looking around as if we are gloating over the damage. You never saw four guys get into a tighter circle in such a hurry when I tell them what we have to do. We'd all heard horrible stories from other Americans about flyers who'd been pitch forked to death by farmers after they parachuted to earth.

Now Sgt. Schmidt orders his soldiers to take positions between the enraged workers and us. Then he shouts, "Halt!" in a stern, commanding voice and the workers do stop coming—just long enough to hear what he is saying. He tells them we have not bombed their city, that we were taken prisoner a month ago in France. He says he is taking us to prison camp, and that he is responsible for our safety. I'm sneaking a peek as he adds, "If you try to harm these men, we will shoot."

Evidently a dozen or so workers either don't believe him or couldn't care less. They start moving toward us again, teeth gritted and hatred blazing in their eyes. The Sergeant orders his men to raise their rifles. As they do, he shouts one last warning at the advancing workers: "Stop! Go back to work or we shoot!" You could see he meant it. The workers, grumbling angrily and shaking their fists at us, finally turn back to their grim tasks. I can feel my heart hammering away after this closest of close calls. *There is not one scintilla of doubt in my mind that the Sergeant saved our lives.* Despite losing his wife in an Allied bombing raid, he had

83

followed his conscience and protected us, as the Geneva Convention on war prisoners says to do. Fortunately for us, both the USA and Germany were signers of that convention. So on this indelible day, four American bomber crewmen would live to tell their grandchildren about a German soldier of honor standing his ground against his own countrymen to save them. How many soldiers under any flag would have had the guts and character to do what he did, especially after losing his wife in the bombing of his home? That man will live on in my heart until it stops beating.

Interrogated By The Enemy

Now Sgt. Schmidt flags down an Army truck that takes us to the interrogation center, some eight miles from town. When I thank him fervently for shielding us from being beaten to death with shovels, he nods and says softly, "It was my duty." The center coming into view as the truck pulls over is a forbidding sight. It is surrounded by twin barbed wire fences, ten feet tall, with rolls of wire in between. Instead of barracks, there are solitary cellblocks for prisoners, and interrogation offices where Germany's best intelligence experts use sophisticated psychological techniques trying to break airmen down so they will tell them whatever they want to know. The interrogators do their best to make each prisoner feel alone, helpless and in fear of his life, regardless of his status as a prisoner of war. The psychological warfare begins with locking us in solitary cells just big enough for a cot. We aren't allowed out unless we have to go to the bathroom or be interrogated, over and over. Even then no prisoner ever catches sight of another. The light bulb in my little space burns brightly 24 hours a day. The cell is deliberately overheated, making a night's sleep difficult if not impossible. I can't even tell day from night because the one tiny window is frosted glass. I have no idea whether I'll be here for a day, a week, a month or even longer.

During the first night I hear tapping on the cell wall and recognize it as dots and dashes of Morse code. I tap back and then listen as the sender claims he is an RAF pilot who's been here for a month. This is really disheartening if true, but I have no way of knowing whether or not this is some psychological trick to break down my morale. What I do know is that I'm better off not believing anything I hear from anyone in this mental pressure cooker. It's standard procedure for interrogators to take each of us aside in turn and ask for much more than the permissible name, rank and serial number. Through cunning, intimidation and bluffing the

Germans occasionally manage to extract usable information from prisoners who are freshly captured and often still in shock.

"We need proof of your identity," they say. "If you can't convince us who you are, we will have to turn you over to the Gestapo as a spy." As we all knew, the murderous Gestapo did indeed shoot airmen who were caught wearing civilian clothes furnished by underground resistance members to help them escape. Soldiers and airmen out of uniform are treated as spies. If a prisoner does tell Luftwaffe questioners anything useful, he might be kept behind here for even more questioning until his information is stale or he was no longer considered of any further value.

These interrogators are adept at putting isolated pieces of information together to learn more than prisoners realize they may be revealing. I am startled during my own interrogation to hear my questioner claim how much he already knows about my group's missions and personnel. For example, he says he knows I flew a recent mission in an aircraft fitted out with highly secret new radar equipment that makes navigation and bombing more accurate in bad weather. This is true! How on earth could he know that? No way, I decide. He's probably bluffing every navigator he questions, hoping to tease out more details about the new equipment. I hadn't been trained yet to use it, so I can't tell him anything useful anyway.

So many Allied airmen are downed at the same time I am that Dulag Luft has to send more and more of us off to prison camp to make room for newcomers. Evidently that is why, after just three days, of solitary, in mid April, I am put on the roster of prisoners going to Stalag Luft I, the largest flying officers prison camp in Germany. It's way up on the Baltic Coast, on a peninsula near the small medieval port of Barth. Life there will be far more exciting than I could have imagined.

85

CHAPTER FIFTEEN

A TRIP TO KRIEGIELAND

The train taking us northeast from Frankfurt to Stalag Luft I on the Baltic Coast near Poland is no Orient Express. It isn't even third class. It has no class at all. We are herded aboard like nervous cattle on their way to a feedlot. But there will be little food where we are going and we will all lose a lot of weight there, not fatten up. By the time guards shove me aboard there are no seats left or even room to lie down somewhere. The only place I can find to sleep is to curl around the toilet. No one else wants to sleep there. The slow, five-day journey is full of abrupt starts, jolting stops and cautious detours around bomb-battered rails. As the train clatters along we pass signs that say, "Raden muessen rollen fuer den Sieg." *Wheels must roll for victory.* But keeping those wheels rolling is obviously a daunting task for track repair workers who are under continual bombardment and fighter attack. Locomotive engineers also have to keep a wary eye on the skies, ready to leap for their lives whenever American P-51's or P-47's suddenly roar in overhead. Our fighter pilots love to strafe railroad steam engines with cannon and machinegun fire that blows them to bits in spectacular explosions. Unfortunately, more than one unmarked train with American prisoners aboard is unwittingly attacked by our fighters, with tragic results. The prisoners on my train are lucky, making the entire trip without coming under "friendly" fire. As

**We new prisoners arrive in
Barth, Germany.**

**Machinegun towers, double barbed wire fencing and
coiled barbed wire between, make Stalag Luft 1
a formidable prison.**

**Map showing where Stalag Luft 1 is located,
far North on the Baltic Coast.**

Unlike us, the guards
were able to dress
for the harsh weather.

we finally pull in at our destination, the little medieval port town of Barth, guards form us into ranks to be marched through town to the camp two miles away.

Townsfolk are lining the streets on this overcast and chilly spring day to watch our sorry parade. I see a pair of matronly hausfraus pointing and laughing as I go by because the back flap of my flyer's plug-in electrically heated garment is hanging down, exposing my bare, goose-pimpled posterior to a brisk and nippy breeze. Rather humiliating, wouldn't you say? How I wish I could plug in and warm up! A Doberman guard dog is right behind me on a handler's leash, ready to clamp his jaws on my chilled cheeks if I don't keep moving.

As we finally reach camp, we can see it's a formidable prison suitable for dangerous criminals. It's surrounded by double rows of barbed wire fencing with an additional barrier of dense coils of barbed wire in between. Guard towers at regular intervals are manned by soldiers with machine guns and searchlights to keep 24-hour watch over every inch of the camp. Additional barbed wire fencing divides the prison into five separate compounds to keep our numbers manageable in case of trouble. Stalag Luft 1 was originally built to house British Airmen, but as more and more Americans were being shot down, the camp was expanded to include us.

As we are marched toward the main gate, hundreds of downed air officers are milling around, jostling for a good look at us and yelling greetings as we march in. "Hey, Parker!" shouts a familiar voice. I scan the crowd and catch sight of my old plane commander, Pete, jumping up and down and waving to get my attention. I feel a rush of joyous relief. Pete's alive! Pete cups his hands and shouts "I'll come over to see you after they assign you guys to a barracks." "Great!" I yell back. At last I'll find out what happened to him and our crew on that disastrous day when they left me behind at the hospital. I end up being assigned to a barracks in North Compound that formerly housed members of the Hitler Youth. Unlike most of the other compounds, it has a mess hall, inside latrines and running water faucets. All compounds also have a church room, theater, library and study room. That's the good news. The bad news is totally inadequate food, clothing and drafty barracks that will keep us very hungry and cold for the dreary months ahead in the icy climate of the Baltic Sea.

Each compound has wooden barracks set up on studs nearly two feet off the ground. Besides making tunneling more difficult, this allows a special guard squad of English-speaking "ferrets" to sneak in underneath at all hours so they can listen for escape plots and other subversive activities. I'm told that one POW retaliated by pouring boiling water down between floor cracks onto a ferret. The German became sizzling mad and emptied his pistol up through the floorboards. Luckily no one was hit. My room is typical, with 14 flying officers crowded into a space about the size of a small living room. The inmates here call themselves "Kriegies," from the German word *Kriegsgefangene* for prisoners of war. Each barracks has double or triple-tiered wooden bunks with wooden slats under burlap mattresses filled with wood chips. As I discover that night, you might as well try to sleep on a sack of gravel.

Look Who's Here!

One of my new roommates is my best wartime buddy, Mike Boomer. I'd gone through pre-flight training with mischievous Mike and last saw him in Pocatello, ID where he trained with another bomb group. He tells me he was shot down on his first mission! His plane exploded with a force that both knocked him unconscious and blew open his parachute. He came to on the ground just inside the Belgian border, and partisans spirited him away before the Germans could find him. Furnished by the Belgian resistance with civilian clothes and knowing just enough French to pose as a local, he managed to get all the way to the Spanish border before the Germans caught him.

I also recognize another bunkmate, the bombardier from my own last mission who shoved my supposedly dead body out of the escape hatch so he could bail out himself. He is Lt. Robert Jones, a husky, 200-pound college grad from Massachusetts. His roommates call him Four Engine Jones to distinguish him from Single Engine Jones, the P-51 pilot in our room. Single Engine's real name is C.L. Jones and he's from Phoenix, Arizona. It takes months for us to get Single Engine Jones to tell us how he got captured. He got lost in bad weather, landed at an airport he thought was in Allied territory—and was promptly taken into custody because it was a German fighter base!

Pete Reveals What Happened to Lonnie

I'm just getting reacquainted with Mike and Four Engine Jones when Pete comes banging through the door and grabs me with a bear hug. He looks older and thinner, but says he didn't suffer a scratch when he bailed out after making sure the rest of the crew hit the silk.

"Parker, you crazy bastard, welcome to the Fatherland," he says. I was hoping you'd show up to keep me company."

"Thanks a lot!" I say. "What happened to the rest of our guys?"

"Everybody made it out okay—except for Lonnie."

"What happened to Lonnie?"

Pete sighs. "His parachute had been ripped up by a cannon shell, so he bailed out with the other waist gunner, hanging onto his web straps. But when the chute popped open, the sudden jolt broke his grip, and...." Pete gestures helplessly. "That was the end of him."

How horrible it must have been for Lonnie, tumbling down for miles toward earth and the certainty of death. I can't help remembering a happier time on our way overseas when Pete detoured to circle our bomber over Lonnie's home in Macon, Georgia. Pete wagged our wings in farewell to Lonnie's mom and dad. Lonnie was always smiling, gentle by nature and easy-going. But now... After a long and awkward silence, Pete claps me on the back in a gesture of comfort. "Well, I guess we can visit more after you get settled," he says. "See you later, buddy—OK?" I nod.

"Thanks for coming by." I say. "It's good to know you're still in one piece." "Likewise," says Pete, and leaves the room.

Fartbrot

Now Mike shows me around and tells me what life is like behind barbed wire. In the center of the room is a squat little stove that burns compressed coal dust briquettes for heating and cooking. "Hey," I say, "you've got a nice little stove here. Keeps you warm, huh?

"Like hell it does!" says Mike. "The coal ration isn't even enough to take the chill off the room." A wooden bench and table with the one and only low-wattage ceiling bulb is the best place to read, Mike says, but it's too chilly to sit there for more than a chapter or two. So you read until you are half-frozen, and then bundle up to get warm in your bunk with your overcoat on—but there's not enough light in your bunk to read by.

Food from the Germans is too skimpy to keep body and soul together. Even with our weekly Red Cross parcels, the dull ache of hunger seldom if ever goes away. Daily rations consist of a few sour slices of black bread adulterated with sawdust; frozen potatoes that you have to cut rotten spots out of, and watery soup with shavings of carrots floating in it. Sometimes we have a thin barley soup and a cup of barley "coffee." The sawdust in the bread is filler to ease hunger pangs, but quite indigestible for anyone but a termite. It causes considerable flatulence, so Kriegies refer to it, indelicately but accurately, as "Fartbrot." Bad as it is, there isn't enough of it. Just a fifth of a loaf per man each day. The bread is dark and heavy as a brick, a wartime mockery of pumpernickel. It has a sour and very unpumpernickl-ish taste.

Here's the actual recipe from the Food Providing Ministry in Berlin:

50% bruised rye grain
20% sliced sugar beets
20% tree flour (sawdust)
10% minced leaves and straw. (That's right, straw!)

Unofficial extra ingredients sometimes found by Kriegies in their brot are bits of glass, wood and sand. The sawdust "tree flour" might well be sweepings from woodworking shops, since it includes some rather large splinters. Splinters and jam, anyone?

There are no fresh fruits or vegetables that I ever get to taste. Sometimes, quite rarely, there's a treat—a glass of beer or a bit of smelly cheese that should be served with a gas mask. But even these humble items disappear as the war grinds on. In fairness, the Germans are hard-pressed for food themselves, but that's no consolation for our ever-shrinking stomachs. Besides, the Germans know that prisoners weakened by hunger are easier to control.

Suppose that you're a healthy male in your twenties. What would usually be uppermost in your mind—young women or food? It was young women, of course, until we got to prison camp. Every morning we wake up hungry. As the stomach-rumbling days dragged by, thoughts of pin-up girls faded and hunger intensified. A formerly overweight gourmet in my room started collecting recipes for breakfasts. Every day he'd sit there on his straw bunk bed with a pencil and paper, imagining breakfasts. He'd smack his lips as he devised every way he could think of to fix eggs, from over easy to Benedict. There'd be crisp bacon. No, sausages. No, a thick slab of Virginia ham! He'd beg the rest of us to tell him of our favorite breakfasts so he could include them in his collection. Finally, I asked him one day, "Why do you torture yourself like this? Are you going to publish a breakfast cookbook when we get out of here?" "Hell, no!" he said. "I'm gonna eat every goddamn one of these breakfasts!"

If it weren't for the International Red Cross, we might be starving like those millions of Jews who died in Nazi concentration camps. Each of

Kriegies delivering that sour-tasting, sawdust adulterated, just plain awful bread we had to eat to avoid starvation.

Potatoes were edible if you cut out the rotten spots, but they were nothing like those tasty Idaho Russets back home.

Stalag Luft 1 photos courtesy of former POW George Luke

us is supposed to receive a weekly Red Cross food parcel. When trains are late and warehouse stocks are exhausted, we do without. *Those Red Cross packages are lifesavers.* They make all the difference in supplying the calories that keep us going. Each contains a can of Spam, a can of dried milk called Klim, which is milk spelled backwards, D-bar chocolate rations, boxes of sugar and raisins, and a can of waxy and utterly tasteless Elgin margarine...yeccch! When I learn that parcels for Canadian prisoners have *real butter* I'm tempted to switch allegiance. Other Kriegies vow that when they get back to the States, they'll bomb that margarine factory. Despite their hunger many prisoners like me just can't gag that margarine down. Instead we burn it for light in makeshift reading lamps made of tin cans with a ribbon of rag for a wick.

Lifting Spirits

Some of the more ingenious Kriegies also contrive to make bootleg booze by fermenting the raisins and sugar in a bucket. This throat-searing stuff has the kick of a bad-tempered elephant at a cheap zoo. It's high-test moonshine. Unfortunately for both the brewers and imbibers, one prisoner with a couple of stiff jolts of raisin jack aboard turns into a Kriegie commando and assaults a guard. He awakens next morning in solitary confinement, suffering the kind of hangover that feels like a head full of razor blades. From then on guards confiscate the raisin rotgut any time they find it.

One quick-witted Kriegie moonshiner, hearing a German raiding party stomping down the hallway, throws his socks into a bucket of freshly made raisin jack and sloshes them up and down as if he were doing his laundry. The raiders barely glance at him as they turn the room upside down and then depart, leaving the bucket of sock-flavored booze untouched. An interesting footnote, pun intended: The socks gave that batch of raisin lightning a linty body and a locker room bouquet.

Besides food and drink, each Red Cross parcel contains a carton of cigarettes, which are the same as money in our cashless prison economy. Non-smokers feed on thinner sinners by bartering their smokes for food. Cigarettes are also invaluable for bribing guards to supply such rare treats as fresh green onions. Once a guard succumbs to bribery, he can be blackmailed for important contraband such as radio parts. The bribing trade falls on hard times, however, when the penalty for guards becomes a transfer to the Russian Front.

The Germans Crack Down

Since the Germans were signers of the 1929 Geneva Convention mandating humane treatment of prisoners, our conditions when I arrived in prison camp were fairly good. But soon after the new Kommandant, Oberst Scherer, a Nazi, authorized guards to use guns to avenge "insults to German honor." New orders regarding air raids required us prisoners to be inside when the "immediate warning" siren was sounded. As a result, several prisoners were fired upon, and one, Lieutenant E. F. "Cisco" Wyman of Maine, was fatally wounded for being outside his barracks during an air raid warning that wasn't even heard by most men in the area. Lt. Wyman had awakened late for church services on Sunday morning, and was on his way when he realized he was all alone out there, and that an air raid alarm must have sounded. As he ran back toward his barracks, a German fence patroller swung his rifle toward him and dropped him with a bullet in the head. Wyman fell in the doorway. Other prisoners pulled him inside and began pounding on the walls and shouting for medical help, but when aid finally came, it was too late.

We prisoners were outraged and lodged protests to the Protecting Powers about these Geneva Convention violations, but without results because Kommandant Scherer refused to forward the correspondence to the neutral authorities in Switzerland. He also became more severe about confining POWs to the "arrest lock"—a jail within the prison —where Kriegies got nothing but bread and water for supposed misbehavior. However when the Protecting Power visited in July, our SAO took the opportunity to bring these violations to the representative's attention. Even though the Kommandant was spoken to severely, it was not until the Protecting Power informed the German Foreign Office, which in turn wrote directly to Oberst Scherer, that Red Cross and personal parcels were allowed in the arrest lock.

CHAPTER SIXTEEN

THE UNDERGROUND NEWS

A few weeks after I arrive at Stalag Luft I, in late April of '44, I'm sum-moned to the room of our Senior American Officer, Colonel J.R. Byerly. As a B-17 group commander before being shot down, the Colonel is our highest-ranking officer. He is slender and of medium height, a soft-spoken gentleman and resolute warrior who is doing a tremendous job in the camp of dealing with our captors. Meanwhile he's also organizing and overseeing our secret activities, from security to tunnel digging.

He gets right to the point. "Lieutenant Parker, I am told you have some newspaper background."

"Yes sir. I wrote stories and articles for the Los Angeles Examiner before the war. I was training to become a reporter."

"We may have an important job for you," the Colonel says. He introduces me to a young American civilian, Lowell Bennett, a war cor-respondent who'd gone along on a mission with a British bomber crew and was shot down over Berlin.

"Lowell started our underground daily newspaper for us, but the Germans are on to him and have threatened to take away his civilian status if he continues his activities."

Lowell nods. "Now that they know what I've been doing, there's no

COLONEL JEAN R. BYERLY

way I can keep the paper going successfully anyhow." (One of the Air Force Captains also suspected of being involved with the paper spent two weeks in the "Cooler"—the camp jail—existing on nothing but bread and water because he insisted he knew nothing about the paper's authors).

Bennett's handwritten daily newspaper was called POW-WOW, an acronym that stands for "Prisoners of War Waiting on Winning." It followed the war's progress each day with information from the BBC in London picked up on our camp's secret radio. "What do you think, Lieutenant?" says the Colonel. "We need someone with newspaper skills to take it over. Would you do this for us?"

"Yes, sir!" I can't imagine a better way to spend all those dreary days ahead in enemy hands and feel useful to my comrades besides. So that's how an apprentice reporter from Los Angeles was promoted to editor-publisher of a paper ultimately circulated daily to nearly nine thousand Allied prisoners. I type it in the Colonel's room on both sides of 8½ by 11 paper, using the typewriter furnished us as required under the Geneva Convention for his communication with neutral authorities in Switzerland.

The Colonel tells me about a radio hidden in the British prisoners' compound. The canny British airmen captured early in the war first bribed and then could blackmail the German guards to furnish the necessary parts and batteries to build a receiver. All the Brits had to do to get whatever they wanted was threaten to betray the guards to their superiors. The guards knew they'd be punished by losing their relatively safe post in camp, be sent to the Russian Front—and probably get killed in combat.

German authorities realized there must be a radio somewhere in camp and kept searching for it, sending a truck with a radio direction finder roaming all around camp. They haven't found it because of the clever way the Brits have set it up, concealed behind a barracks wall. Connecting a short wire between two nail heads on the wall is all it takes to turn it on for the BBC's 11:30 a.m. and 10 p.m. newscasts. The wire is quickly disconnected after each broadcast, leaving no external clue to the radio itself.

Col. Byerly explains that POW-WOW has become vital to camp morale because our men are so anxious to know what's really happening in the war, and how soon they might go home again. Unless we have a trustworthy news source of our own, we'll be at the mercy of rumors that spread like wildfire, sending spirits soaring one day and plummeting the next. All the Nazi newspapers supplied to us put a propaganda spin on the military communiqués. Broadcasts made in German each day over speakers in our barracks, are suspect for the same reason. German citizens and everyone else in Occupied Europe are strictly forbidden to listen to the British newscasts.

We resume publication of POW-POW as soon as strict and elaborate new security arrangements are completed for distributing the paper. I move into our headquarters barracks, known as the "head shed," with three other volunteers who join POW-WOW's secret staff: Major Don Ross, a gifted sketch and cartoon artist who draws our maps and headlines; and two Kriegies who understand German, Lieutenants A. B. Austin of Long Beach, California and E. H. Gallagher of Newark, New Jersey. Austin and Gallagher translate the German papers, "Der Angriff" (The Attack) and "Der Volkische Beobachter" (The People's Observer) as well as the daily radio Der Wehrmacht (Supreme Army Command).

A Wad of Secrets

Preparation for each day's issue begins when British Warrant Officer R. R. Drummond appears at my "office." As someone who distributes music recordings and games throughout camp, Drummond has access to all the compounds. What he brings me each day is a wad of toilet paper concealed in his hollow wristwatch. It's a penciled transcription of the BBC's noon broadcast. Although the toilet tissue is of poor quality, stiff and shiny like butcher's paper, it's just the thing for penciled notes. Drummond tells me he is occasionally patted down and searched, but the guards haven't caught on to that watch with no works inside. Even if they do glance at it, Drummond is always careful beforehand to set it for the right time of day. Thanks to Officer Drummond I can now compare the BBC news with the information Austin and Gallagher glean from the German sources. I soon discover how useful these comparisons can be. British communiqués always tell us where Allied troops are moving forward. The Germans always emphasize where their troops are holding ground. When I match these reports against one another, a remarkably accurate picture emerges of what is actually going on.

Some Kriegies think we are just rehashing the German newspapers, but we aren't. Our readers are getting the news as fast as anyone else in the world, and more complete and accurate than what the Germans are allowed to read from their own sources. We were actually able to give the prisoners the news about the liberation of Paris two hours before New York heard about it.

I'd only been editing POW-WOW for about three months when a story broke that we'd all been waiting for, but I didn't dare tell anybody about it! Why? Because if we didn't wait to break the story though POW-WOW, under tight security inside each barracks, it would have been all over camp in a few minutes, and might have blown our cover when the Germans saw all the excitement and hullabaloo. I should have known from the broad smile on Warrant Officer Drummond's face that there was big news on that little piece of toilet paper he gave me. It was the BBC's story the whole free world was waiting for: The invasion of Europe on D-Day, June 8, 1944. By the time POW-WOW was circulated in mid-afternoon, the German radio in our barracks hallway was broadcasting the German version of the Invasion, so no suspicions were aroused.

How It Was Done

To start writing each daily edition of POW-POW I feed four sheets of paper plus carbons into the Colonel's typewriter. Then I bang those keys as hard as I can, condensing the most important information into news stories in dual columns on both sides of the paper, complete with headlines and datelines. Needless to say, there are never any bylines or mentions of our little band of conspirators behind the headlines.

Copies are circulated throughout camp in the greatest secrecy. Some go by "Kriegie airmail," stuffed into an empty dried milk can and tossed over the fence when guards aren't watching to a waiting confederate in the next compound. One compound on the other side of the German headquarters gets special delivery by a postal officer, J.K. Lash, who carries a copy tucked between his teeth and cheek. If he runs into trouble, he is to chew it up. I'm glad he goes undiscovered and doesn't have to eat my words.

With our own guards posted on alert for those English-speaking German "ferrets," the paper is read softly aloud to small groups in each room and then passed to the next. When the entire barracks has heard the news, the paper is either forwarded to another compound or burned to ashes to avoid leaving evidence. This system works so well that we get cocky that summer and add a Sunday supplement with features and commentary submitted by other prisoners. At POW-WOW's circulation peak near war's end, we were reaching an estimated 9,000 captured Americans, British, Canadians and other nationalities with editions in three languages—English, French and Russian.

101

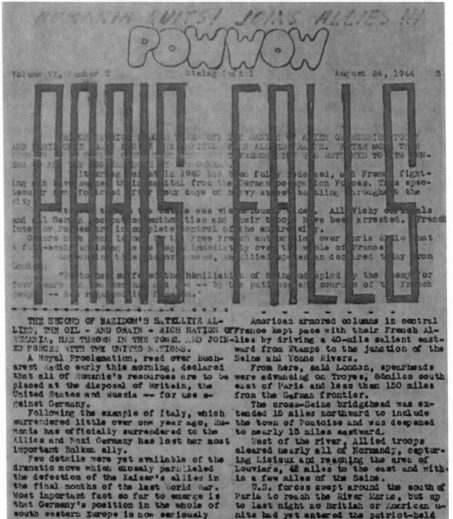

**POW – WOW on
the Liberation of Paris from the Germans.**

Cartoon courtesy of USAF Major General Don Ross

POW – WOW for D-Day.

CHAPTER SEVENTEEN

A DAY IN THE LIFE

ife in Stalag Luft I turns out to be mostly dreary monotony with un-varying sameness, day after depressing day. Each morning begins with guards stomping through the hallways, beating on doors and routing us out of bed by shouting 'Alles 'raus!" (Everybody out!) We come stumbling out, half awake, to form up in ranks so the guards can count us off and make sure no one has escaped during the night. Meanwhile other guards are checking the barracks for anyone ill or lagging behind, which changes the numbers. Winter mornings are the worst. We are poorly clad to withstand the icy Baltic winds. It's the worst winter in 50 years, and it's colder than a polar bear's backside. If the guards bungle the count and the totals don't match up, as happens all too often, we just have to stand there, shivering, shuffling our feet, and flapping our arms to keep the blood circulating while they count all over again. We aren't much better off when roll call finally ends because our rooms are like walk-in freezers.

Summer is far more pleasant. Sunshine thaws us out and we enjoy such meager pleasures as playing basketball under the machine guns of the guard towers above us. There's a special rule for these games, and we'd better remember it: if the ball rolls inside the "dead line," a single strand of warning wire in front of the barbed wire fences, you

Kriegies line up for roll call on a cold winter's day.

**Stalag Luft 1 barrack and guard tower.
In the background can be seen St. Mary's church
in Barth, visible to all the prisoners.**

Kriegies at Stalag Luft 1 relax playing basketball..

**Stalag Luft 1 POWs enjoy the musical performance
of the Kriegie band.**

must ask permission to retrieve it or you can be shot without warning. Another popular activity in our captive community is getting exercise by walking brisk laps within the limits of our separate compounds. I'm a lap walker whenever weather permits. My favorite way to spend wintry days is indoors playing bridge, taught in the Culbertson bidding style by Four Engine Jones, the bombardier who shoved my supposedly dead body out the nose hatch so he could bail out. We play so often that we literally wear the suits and numbers right off the cards. Unable to get another deck, we improvise by restoring them as best we can with red and black ink. We don't play for money because all we have in our pockets is lint, so the usual stakes are cigarettes from our Red Cross packages.

A few prisoners with special duties are allowed to visit all compounds to distribute that precious rarity called mail, or to circulate music recordings and board games. I'd been thinking of using my time behind barbed wire to improve my knowledge of conversational German, but I have to abandon that idea after becoming the editor of "POW-WOW," which requires my keeping a low profile to avoid attracting any attention.

The Spike Jones Polka

Grim though the life here can be, there are often lighter moments of fun and irrepressible Kriegie mischief bubbling up to raise morale. There was a middle-aged little Austrian guard who kept telling us that he wasn't a German, apparently trying to ingratiate himself. A naturally friendly fellow, he liked to play his concertina for us. One day a Kriegie taught him a polka he'd never heard before, and we all gathered to enjoy it. In fact the Kriegies came running as they heard him start playing. The applause was tremendous. He was a star! But the next day he came around with a reproachful look and said we'd taught him a bad song that got him into trouble. It was Spike Jones' wartime comedy song about Hitler, "Der Fuehrer's' Face." It began like this:

"When der Fuhrer says vee are the master race,
Vee heil, heil, right in der Fuhrer's face.
Not to love der Fuhrer is a great disgrace,
So vee heil, heil, right in der Fuhrer's face!"

Kriegies looked for mischief wherever they could find it, just for fun. When the guards came through our rooms to replace our inadequate ceiling lights with even smaller wattages, a couple of Kriegies followed them at a discreet distance, putting the better lights back in their sockets.

108

Hearing From Home

Mail Call causes the most excitement among us lonely young guys so many thousands of miles from home. It takes an average of seven months for letters or packages to reach us, and months more for our letters to reach our families. Mail follows an extremely slow, bureaucratic path in and out of censorship before and after distribution through neutral authorities. A letter I get from mom says dad took to bed the day I was reported missing in action, and didn't get up until the Air Force sent word nearly three months later that I was a prisoner. The family also sends me a birthday cake that I share with my roommates, as is the custom. Cookies and other baked goodies we receive don't last long, even though we eat them ever so slowly, savoring their taste to the last fragrant crumb. Most letters from home tell of family doings and concerns about our welfare as prisoners. Other letters I hear about are collectors' items, like these:

"Dear Nephew, I'm enclosing a calendar. Thought it would come in handy, as it has several years on it."

And this one: "Dearest, when you get back I would like a divorce. I'm living with a cadet in Santa Ana, California and I'd like to marry him. He's a wonderful fellow and I know you would like him."

Another great pleasure for all of us is the occasional swing band concert featuring Kriegie musicians playing instruments supplied by the YMCA. They play really well together, swinging the favorites we danced to before our wings were clipped. Hearing these familiar melodies is a bittersweet experience, evoking happy memories but making us more homesick than ever.

CHAPTER EIGHTEEN
THE DEFIANT COLONEL SPICER

One of the most colorful characters in camp is Col. Henry "Russ" Spicer, former commander of the 375th Fighter Group of P-51 Mustangs. He sports a huge RAF-style handlebar mustache, and is never without his pipe. He was shot down by flak over the French coast on March 3rd, 1944 when he went down to 7,000 feet so as to light that pipe. He bailed out into the freezing waters of the English Channel and drifted for two days in a one-man dinghy. Rescue boats and aircraft couldn't find him. His feet and hands were badly frostbitten when he finally drifted ashore near Cherbourg, France. Unable to walk and near collapse, he was found lying on the beach by German soldiers. He was still suffering from frostbite when he arrived at our camp.

Col. Spicer had an outspoken contempt for his captors that nearly cost him his life. While Senior American Officer in North Compound 2, he infuriated the Germans by giving this speech at a roll call formation, on October 31, 1944:

"Yesterday, an officer (Major Bronson) was put in the cooler for two weeks. He had two counts against him. The first, failure to obey the order of a German officer, is beside the point. The second was failure to salute a German officer of lower rank. The Articles of the Geneva Convention say to salute all officers of equal or higher rank. The Germans in this camp

COLONEL HENRY "RUSS" SPICER,
in the cockpit of his P-51 Mustang, "Tony Boy".

**The prisoner jail at Stalag Luft 1 housed the defiant
Colonel Spicer until the very end of the war.**

have put out an order that we must salute all German officers whether lower or higher rank. My order to you is salute all German officers of equal or higher rank. I have noticed that many of you are buddy-buddy with the Germans. Remember that we are still at war with the Germans. They are still our enemies and are doing everything they can to win this war. Don't let him fool you around this camp, because he is a dirty lying sneak and can't be trusted. As an example of the type of enemy you have to deal with, the British were forced to retreat in the Arnheim area. They had to leave the wounded in the hospital. The Germans took the hospital and machine-gunned all those British in their beds. In Holland, behind the German lines, a woman with a baby in her arms was walking along the road evacuating the battle zone. Some British prisoners were passing her. She gave them the "V" for victory sign. A German soldier saw her and without hesitation swung his gun around and shot her on the spot. They are a bunch of murderous no-good liars and if we have to stay here for 10 years to see all the Germans killed then it will be worth it."

Loud cheers are heard from the men. The Colonel then turns to the German Major and Non-Coms standing at the side and says. "For your information, these are my personal opinions and I'm not attempting to incite riot or rebellion. They are my opinions and not necessarily the opinions of the men." More loud cheers. Then facing the men again he said, "That is all, men, and remember what I have told you."[5] Within hours the Colonel was in solitary confinement. He was court-martialed on trumped-up charges of rebellion and sentenced to death to take effect in six months.

Nothing could break his spirit. When Kriegies under guard were walked past the building where he was held in solitary, they'd shout words of encouragement. The Colonel would shout back, "Keep fighting! Don't give in to the bastards!" Asked if he needed anything, he always replied, "Yeah, send me machine guns!" Sentenced to death by firing squad, he escaped execution as the war was ending by the narrowest of margins, a single day!

CHAPTER NINETEEN
THE BIG BET

Morale in our camp is high in September '44, and with good cause. On the Western front, Paris has just been liberated by Free French, USA and British forces, and American troops are now assaulting Nazi Germany's fortified Siegfried Line, a defensive wall of pillboxes. Meanwhile the Soviets continue to push the Germans back from Eastern Europe, liberating Bucharest, the capital of Romania.

Some Kriegies at Stalag Luft I even dare to think they might be home by Christmas. That's what leads to the big bet in North Compound 2 between an optimist, Lt. Richard D. Stark of Tampa, Florida, and a pessimist, 2nd. Lt. Stanley M. Johnson of Port Allegany, Pennsylvania. We prisoners have no money or possessions to wager, so Lt. Stark tells pessimist Johnson, "If we aren't home by Christmas, I will kiss your a** before the whole group formation on Christmas morning." They shake hands and the bet is on.

Clearly the Germans are losing the war and being pushed back into their own country, but they aren't through yet. Hitler, who survived an assassination attempt in a failed coup on July 20th, still hopes to negotiate peace with the Western allies so he can carry on the war against the Soviets in the East.

Just ten days before Christmas, British Officer Drummond hands

"The Only Truthful Newspaper in Germany"

POW WOW

Volume VI, Number 24   Stalag Luft I   September 16,

SIEGFRIED BREACHED

ALLIED SUPREME HQ., SEPTEMBER 15...........Yank fighting-men burst through the vaunted Siegfried Defense Line on the German frontier yesterday, shattering its chain of gun emplacements and encircling the city of Aachen, announced Gen. Eisenhower's Headquarters. Naziism's last perimeter defense has been breached. The road to the Rhine and Hitler's industry-packed Ruhr lies before our armies.

* * * * * * * * * * * * * *

GREAT NEW LANDINGS IN PACIFIC

Pacific Hq., Sept. 15............American amphibious forces struck westward towards the Philippines today with two great landings on Palau and Yap Islands. Latest battleships of the U. S. Navy covered and prepared the landings, disclosed a communique from the joint headquarters of General Douglas MacArthur and Admiral Chester Nimitz.

The Japs were reportedly taken completely by surprise and initial losses were described as very light. No planes or ships were lost during the first 12 hours of the landings.

Admiral Chester Nimitz' Marine forces went ashore on Palau and Yap Islands, 1,200 and 750 miles respectively from our latest landings on Guam Island.

Simultaneously, U. S. Army forces went ashore on Maroti Island and Hemla-Hara, both further west towards the Philippines.

A naval and air assault unparalleled in the Pacific to date heralded the new amphibious operations. Five hundred Jap planes were destroyed and 173 vessels sunk or badly damaged in the terrific air-sea hammering preceding the landings.

Included in naval squadrons supporting the operation, disclosed Washington, were America's latest battleships of the Wisconsin Class (57,000 tons).

The new landings brought American troops to less than a thousand miles from Manila, scene of military disasters in the first days of the war. The Japanese hold on the Caroline Islands, including the naval base at Truk, is now completely encircled and our forces have jumped half-way to the Dutch East Indies.

American tank spearheads, under a sky dark with aerial artillery, punched thru the network of pill-boxes, traps and gun emplacements southeast of Aachen and nullified in a day the whole Nazi defense system on the western frontier.

Simultaneously, British and American divisions rumbled into Germany at a new point, capturing the Belgian city of Maasticht and crossing the border north of Aachen.

By nightfall, these forces were ... miles inside the Reich and had linked up with U. S. units east of Aachen to encircle the city.

Allied Headquarters announced that our forces were on the outskirts of the city and London military observers declared its fall to be imminent.

The Gestapo has fled from this area, added front reports, and the Allied Military Government has already moved in and is in operation.

Along the Moselle front U. S. 3rd Army forces pushed forward to even out an inward bulge in our line. One column has driven 37 miles during the past two days from Neufchateau to capture Epinal in the Vosges Mountains.

Another force, using the bridge-head across the Moselle as a starting point, moved 16 miles southeast of Nancy to the area of Luneville where strength is being built up to cross the Meurthe River.

The gains on this sector lengthened the Allied front along the Moselle River to 150 miles, from immediately west of Trier to Epinal. Moreover, the German 19th Army was further threatened on its right flank by our southward driving columns.

In the northernmost Belgium, British and Army forces moved across the Scheldt

[continued top col. 1 page 5]

POW - WOW announcing that the Allies had broken through the Germans' supposedly impenetrable defenses and were now moving into Germany.

116

me our daily handwritten transcript of the BBC war news. One brief little item catches my eye because it's puzzling. It says that a German plane had been sighted over our lines in the Ardennes Forest along the Belgian-German border. I look at our homemade maps, which have pins representing troop positions, and I realize our lines are stretched quite thinly there. Evidently our forces are not expecting German activity in that heavily forested region during some of the coldest, snowiest weather in half a century. Yet within 24 hours, the Germans launch an all-out-attack there with more than half a million men, achieving complete surprise. The news devastates camp morale, which hits bottom as the battle rages on. Obviously the Germans have far more fight left in them than we thought!

The goal of three powerful German Armies in that mighty, all-out assault is to reach the sea, trap four allied armies, and force the negotiated peace Hitler wants on the western front. The Battle of the Bulge, which lasts from December 16, 1944 to January 28, 1945, develops into the largest land battle the United States has ever fought. More than a million men are involved—600,000 Germans, 500,000 Americans and 55,000 British. Casualties number over 81,000 U.S., including 19,000 killed in action; 1,400 British with 200 killed, and 100,000 Germans killed, wounded or captured. Our losses include 82 POW's machine-gunned down in cold blood by fanatical Nazi SS troops at Malmedy.

Although we Kriegies don't realize it at the time, the desperate go-for-broke German attack that fails with such heavy losses of men and equipment will accelerate their final defeat, less than four months later, on V-E day, May 8, 1945.

Meanwhile, true to his word, our own Lt. Stark has a debt to pay on Christmas Day. All 1,500 prisoners in North Compound 2 are still drawn up in formation after the morning head-count as Stark comes front and center, carrying a bucket of warm water, a bar of soap and a towel. Waiting for him is the wager winner, Lt. Johnson, who drops his pants and bends over, mooning the assemblage. While German officers watch in astonishment, Stark washes and pats dry one of Johnson's bare cheeks, and then plants a kiss on it! The assembled POW's erupt in mighty cheers.

A few days later, the Germans relax their rules for the holiday so we can move around freely to visit friends in other compounds. Our leaders order distribution of an extra Red Cross parcel to each of us to celebrate Christmas. One of the Kriegies that evening begins singing "Silent Night," and the guards join in the familiar carol, which originated in Germany as

117

"Stille Nacht, Heilige Nacht." Lonely and homesick as we prisoners are on this terribly cold night, we are comforted by the thought that the war is nearing its end. Next Christmas we'll surely be free, celebrating with our loved ones at home.

CHAPTER TWENTY

A LEADER
FOR DESPERATE TIMES

Col. Hubert "Hub" Zemke was one of the best fighter pilots and group commanders in the entire Eighth Air Force. He was aggressive, stubborn, demanding, impetuous and sometimes in hot water with the brass, but his men would follow him anywhere and he led them brilliantly. As a premier ace, he commanded the famed 56th Fighter Group, known as 'Zemke's Wolfpack,' which flew P-47 Thunderbolts and broke all records for German planes destroyed in the air.[6] After he had flown an impressive 450 combat hours, the VIII Fighter Command concludes it's time for him to join their headquarters staff, "flying a desk." But the independent-minded Zemke decides to fly one more mission on October 30, 1944, before reporting as ordered, and his luck runs out when a wing comes off as he's trying to dodge a storm. Injured while bailing out, he is in shock and dazed as he lands in a forest south of Hanover, Germany. His right arm is so swollen he fears it's broken, so he uses his escape knife to cut a panel from the chute for a sling. Walking is painful with a sore leg, and the side of his face is swelling. Almost exhausted and unable to run when surprised by a group of armed villagers, he has to surrender. It helps in this dicey situation as well as in prison camp later that he's of German descent and speaks the language fairly well. Zemke comes close to death again when an Allied fighter plane strafes the train

119

taking him to our camp. Bullets thud into the compartment where he's sitting with his guards, narrowly missing him but killing a young German girl sitting opposite him.

When Zemke reaches Stalag Luft I in November 1944 and has a reunion with old buddies, they compare notes and discover that he is the most senior in rank. And that means—surprise!—that he will be taking over as Senior American Officer, responsible for the welfare of some 5,000 prisoners. Colonel J. R. Byerly, our commander who'd done such an effective job organizing us as a cohesive unit, is ready to turn over his duties because of poor health. He's plagued by a chronic liver ailment that's being aggravated by harsh camp conditions—including lack of a special diet and medicines he needs and doesn't get.

Zemke soon learns that we Kriegies are organized in Air Force fashion under our own Provisional Wing X, which officially represents us to the Germans but is also deeply involved in secret underground operations. Everything is on a "need to know" basis so that as few men as possible know about such activities as efforts to escape. Those of us on POW-WOW's staff have no idea who is digging tunnels where or when, and the escape experts don't know anything useful to the Germans about how we get and publish the news. Even Zemke doesn't know (because he doesn't want to) about how POW-WOW operates until the end of the war. The less anyone knows, the better.

Special guards who understand English are constantly snooping around, hoping to uncover any "verboten" secret operations. Our defense is to post our own guards who yell "Goon up!" when they spot them. ("Goon" refers to a weird female character from outer space in the American "Popeye" comic strip of the Forties.) Guards sometimes ask, "What's a goon?" but they don't like the answer.

Cloak And Dagger Stuff

Escape attempts are ongoing projects, despite the unfortunate fact that our camp is built on sandy soil. Tunneling takes endless shoring up with the only wood available—our bed slats—to keep them from collapsing. Month after month tunnels are dug by hungry and exhausted men, only to be discovered at the last possible moment. Eventually we realize the Germans must be using sensors that detect digging sounds. They're playing cat and mouse with us, letting our men tunnel as far as the fence before they move in to stop us. We have the last laugh, however, because

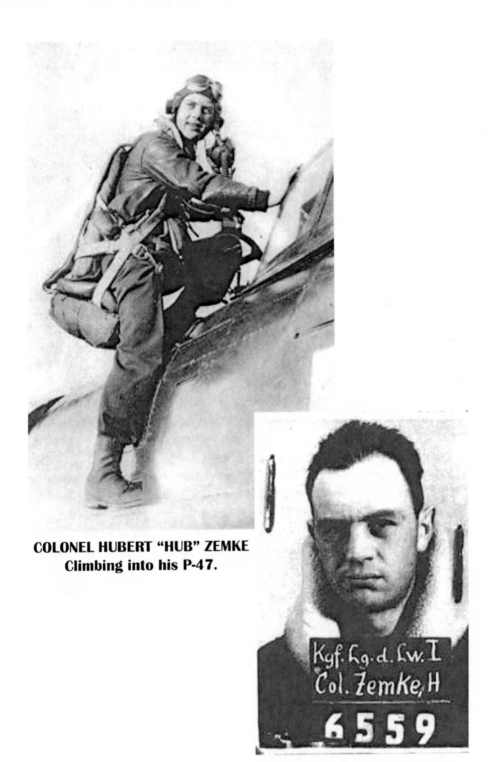

COLONEL HUBERT "HUB" ZEMKE
Climbing into his P-47.

Stalag Luft 1 prison photo.

121

one tunnel, built late in the war for emergencies only, goes undetected. By this time the Germans probably want to escape themselves.

Our own experts also keep busy forging identity and travel documents and making maps for likely escape routes. These are surprisingly well crafted with exquisite skill to deceive any inspectors. Chances of getting out of Germany undetected are slim, however, since our camp on the Baltic Coast near Poland is far from Allied lines. I don't know to this day of any escape attempt from our camp that succeeded for more than a few hours.

We also have a secret commando unit for self-defense, trained by a British Army expert and armed with crude homemade weapons stashed away underground. They are readying for the day they may have to surprise patrolling guards and seize their weapons before machine gunners in the watchtowers realize what's happening.

As the new American Senior Officer, Zemke is greatly concerned about keeping us safe during the coming chaos when the German military machine finally collapses. There's no way to predict what will happen. Some fanatical Nazi SS unit might want to wreak vengeance on we airmen who have laid waste their country. There's a rumor that Hitler, raving in frustration as German troops are driven back on all fronts, has ordered the slaughter of all Allied flyers in prison camps. We know from a steady flow of incoming prisoners that enlisted airmen in camps further east, like Stalag Luft IV in Poland, have already suffered great hardship. They were evacuated ahead of the advancing Russians and forced to march west for 86 days without proper food, clothing or medicine under absolutely unspeakable conditions. Several die on that exhausting and utterly miserable journey of starving, half-frozen prisoners who were also sickened by the hundreds. Whatever else happens, Zemke is resolved that we in our thousands at Stalag Luft I will rise in rebellion against any order to march us out of camp, away from food supplies and shelter in the teeth of this terrible winter.

Echoes Of The Holocaust

Meanwhile, Zemke must deal with a more immediate problem—the special peril faced by American POW's of Jewish descent. One of them, Aaron Kuptsow, tells what happened in our camp on a February morning in 1945 at roll call: "The German Officer called out a bunch of our names and told us to remain after dismissal. After the others left, we were marched through camp to another barracks and told that this was our new home. I was in a room with thirteen others, and after talking for a few minutes, we realized that we were all Jewish. We checked the other rooms and realized that everyone in our barracks was Jewish. It was in a distant corner of camp, surrounded by barbed wire and isolated. Rumors started to spread that we would probably be marched out some night and sent to death camps, and no one would know." The men decide to contact the Geneva Convention authorities through our Senior American Officer, Col. Zemke.

"To this day," says Kuptsow, "I believe that the strength and sheer guts of Col. Zemke and Col. Spicer, who told the German Commandant that this was a violation of the Geneva Convention, and that a protest would be filed and given to the international inspectors were what saved us. In addition, the action by the Nazis was a crime against American Officers and they were being persecuted for their religious beliefs. Col. Zemke told the Germans they would be held responsible when the war was over. The situation was resolved when Col. Zemke arranged for us to be moved to the barracks where he had his headquarters." It reminded me of Mike Encinias' story of the Nazi who refused to question him directly because Mike has brown skin and, in the guard's eyes must therefore be inferior to all Germans. So instead, the Nazi relayed his questions to Mike via another prisoner with the Aryan look of blond hair and blue eyes, unaware that Mr. Blue Eyes was...Jewish!

Facing Starvation

One problem that keeps frustrating Col. Zemke's best efforts is obtaining enough food for increasing thousands of prisoners to stave off constant hunger. The problem is growing even worse as the German rail system, greatly overburdened and constantly under attack, becomes all but paralyzed. While a square meal is something we can only dream about - and we do - the food shortage that intensifies in the fall of 1944 raises the specter of starvation. Our "normal" ration of German food, 1200 to 1800 calories a day, drops steadily until it bottoms out at a mere 800 calories. Shipments of Red Cross parcels are dwindling, forcing rationing to half parcels per week. There's a temporary increase to full parcels in December – including an extra for Christmas—but as the New Year be-gins, deliveries are slashed again. We're back on half-rations in January and February, losing weight we just can't afford. We're becoming skin and bone.

Morale hits an all-time low toward the end of March, when no parcels are distributed all month! Evidently trains carrying our Red Cross parcels are not getting through, and our cupboard is bare. German food is also deteriorating to the point we are literally starving. Men become so weak they fall down while trying to get out of bed or when standing up too quickly. Some have to help others make it to roll call. One prisoner who just got a postcard from home saying he's the father of twins runs to my barracks to have POW-WOW spread the happy news—and collapses on the floor at my feet. Some men get so desperate that our senior officers assign others to stand guard over garbage cans to prevent scavenging for scraps that will only make the scavengers sick.

Finally the German authorities agree to Col. Zemke's outraged insistence that they permit Sweden, a neutral Protecting Power like Switzerland, to ship us American Red Cross parcels across the Baltic. We provide Kriegies as drivers on parole to make collection runs to the port of Lubeck, in trucks painted white with Red Cross markings to help ward off possible strafing by Allied fighters.[7] Overnight we go from starving to rejoicing that the warehouse is now stocked with nourishing Red Cross food that should keep us going, still hungry but not starving, on a parcel a week for another couple of months.

CHAPTER TWENTY-ONE

BYE-BYE, POW-WOW

The end for POW-WOW comes suddenly in early April 1945, after a year of successful operation. A German Sergeant enters my room, salutes and says "Leutnant Parker, Herr Kommandant wishes to see you." Uh-oh! The Germans finally have my number. I follow the Sergeant to Camp Headquarters where our newest Kommandant, Col. Von Warnstedt is lounging back casually with his shiny black boots up on his desk, blowing a smoke ring. It's like a scene from a movie. "Cigarette?" he asks politely, pushing his pack across the desk. I can see they are Sports, a fake German brand with no tobacco and an aroma like a brush fire.

"No thanks," I say, thinking I'd rather spend a week in solitary than inhale one of those dreadful wartime smokes. I'm tempted to offer him an American cigarette—the kind made with real tobacco—but this is no time to be insulting the camp commander.

He takes a deep drag and blows another smoke ring, obviously savoring this moment, if not that cigarette. He gives me an amused smile and then gets down to business.

"Leutnant Parker," he says softly in accented English, "We know what you have been doing, and we have sent your records to Berlin. When they come back, we will know what to do with you. You are dismissed."

I had expected a real grilling, followed by being tossed into solitary like all the other prisoners caught disobeying German regulations. Why would he dismiss me without asking a single question? Why wouldn't he want to know the names of everyone involved with POW-WOW unless he already knew everything? This was far too easy.

The waiting Sergeant gestures toward the door. I exchange salutes with the Kommandant and follow the Sergeant back to my room. I don't sleep very well that night because I have no idea how severe my punishment will be. Maybe I'll get off with a term in solitary on bread and water. Then again, I might be put on trial and sentenced to be shot, like Col. Spicer.

Whatever the penalty could have been, I'll never know. The papers didn't come back from Berlin. Or if they did, the Kommandant ignored them because the war was nearing its end anyway. Or perhaps he never did report me to the higher authorities in Berlin. I doubt he saw any point in punishing American prisoners during these final days of the Third Reich.

The morning after my puzzling encounter with the Kommandant, he tells the guards at their morning formation about the demise of POW-WOW and what I'd been doing. As soon as he dismisses them, several run across the yard to my barracks window, asking, "Leutnant Parker, was sind die Nachrichten? (What are the news reports?)"

The game is up, so I tell them what's happening in their collapsing country. Thanks to those wily Brits and their secret radio, we POWs had always known more about the war than most Germans did.

CHAPTER TWENTY-TWO

AS WAR NEARS END, WHAT FATE AWAITS US?

By the spring of 1945, Nazi Germany is sliding into the chaos of defeat. American and British troops are advancing rapidly though the German heartland after crossing the Rhine, and the Russians are besieging Berlin. That's the good news. But what will become of us 9,000 prisoners at Stalag Luft I, directly in the path of fast moving Soviet troops? Will our German guards try to force us to march west at great personal risk and hardship to escape the Russians? If not, will the Russians liberate us as brothers in arms and set us free, or ship us back to the Soviet Union to be pawns in their already difficult dealings with the Western Allies? There's even a possibility that fanatical Nazi SS troops, reliably reported nearby, might act on Hitler's orders to slaughter all of us "Luftgangsters" who bombed their country into rubble. All such dire possibilities weigh on the mind of Col. Zemke, who is responsible for preparing us for whatever might happen and for dealing with rapidly developing events.

Meanwhile, the sad news reaches us via the BBC that President Franklin D. Roosevelt has died. The guards are surprised to hear Kriegies talking about FDR's loss because they haven't heard the news yet. Obviously we have a secret radio, but they still can't find it.

Defying The Germans

Late in April, Col. Zemke receives a message to report to the Kommandant's office. As Zemke writes in his wartime memoir, "Zemke's Stalag," von Warnstedt reads him a teletype order from Supreme German Headquarters that "set my hair on end." All German personnel and prisoners of war are to be ready to evacuate Stalag Luft I within 24 hours notice, moving west to the Hamburg area. As the meeting ends, Zemke makes plain his "lack of enthusiasm" for the move. Doing this at the eleventh hour in near chaos would surely put many lives at risk.

Back in his room, he convenes a meeting of his staffers with British senior officers participating. Everyone is aghast to hear the news. We have ample Red Cross parcels stored here to feed all 9,000 of us for the time being, but it would be a senseless risk for us to go marching off in winter weather without adequate transport and supplies. Zemke calls on his senior officers and the British leaders for a vote by secret ballot and the result is a firm "stay put!" Our Kriegie commandos are alerted and London notified by radio transmission of our intentions. (I hadn't known we were in touch with London because our having acquired a transmitter was a big secret and was on a "need to know" basis only, and I obviously didn't "need" to know.) Zemke decides to go back to von Warnstedt immediately to face him "with no evasion or false diplomacy." Zemke tells him that all our senior officers and all prisoners object to forced evacuation and insist on staying in camp until the war ends. An informant we have in von Warnstedt's office soon tells us that he's spoken to the German High Command headquarters, reporting that the prisoners object to moving and that he lacks the men and transport to accomplish it. Clearly the Kommandant has no more enthusiasm for this forced evacuation of thousands of prisoners at this time than we do.

Meanwhile, Zemke designates three teams of senior officers to head for the American, British and Soviet lines to make contact and help arrange our evacuation. They all get through the chaotic German countryside to make their contacts, and soon preparation for an airlift to freedom is under way in France.

Adolph Hitler Ends It All

As April ends, word came from our BBC radio that Adolph Hitler committed suicide in his Berlin bunker that was under siege by Russian troops.

**Kommandant Von Warnstedt (2nd from right, front row)
and his staff of Stalag Luft I.**

Guard tower in the deadly winter snow.
(inset of nearby forest)

Our German radios in each barracks hallway play funereal dirges for hours before the announcement that "Unser Fuhrer ist tot." (Our leader is dead.) Next morning the Kommandant summons Col. Zemke to tell him "The war is now over for us."

The Kommandant asks if our Senior American officers could take over the camp and permit all German personnel to leave peacefully without bloodshed. As Zemke says in his memoir, "I could not have wished to hear sweeter words. My reply was a firm 'yes,' provided all his troops left together, took only small arms for personal protection, and did not attempt to destroy any of the camp facilities." Von Warnstedt agrees. He and his departing troops will assemble outside the camp at midnight, leaving the gates open and the prisoners free. He also agrees to the wisdom of Zemke's request that German personnel not inform the prisoners in advance. Zemke fears, with good reason, that this might create pandemonium, with some unruly elements running amok and jeopardizing the whole effort to have a bloodless takeover by seeking revenge on some unpopular guards.

The departure of the guards at midnight goes smoothly. Von Warnstedt and Zemke exchange salutes, the dejected German officer says "Auf Wiedersehen," and walks off to the sedan that will carry him west to surrender to the Allies.

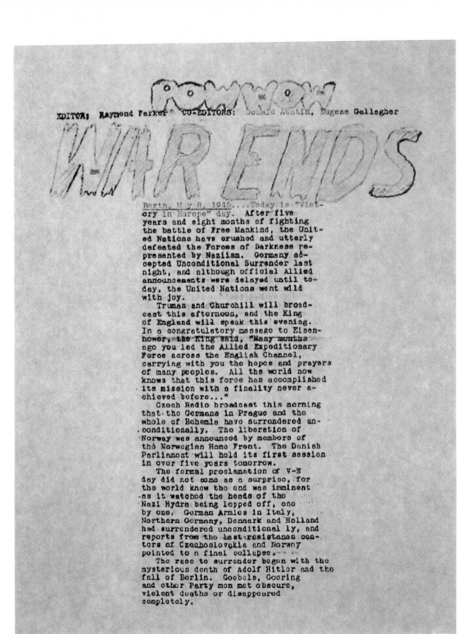

POW – WOW

Finally, Ray is able to put his name on the masthead, with the other brave men who assisted in writing the underground paper.

CHAPTER TWENTY-THREE

THE RUSSIANS ARE COMING

Next morning, early in May, we awake to see there are no guards in the gun towers. There are no guards anywhere! And wonderful to behold, the Stars and Stripes and the Union Jack are fluttering side by side in a pleasant breeze. The flags were made in secret by Kriegies and hidden away to be flown on this day. We soon learn how the Germans quietly abandoned our camp around midnight and fled to the West, terrified at falling into the hands of the advancing Russians. They offered guns to our leaders for defense against the Russians, thinking them little more than savages—"uncultiviert." Considering the savage way German troops treated the Russian people after invading the USSR, they had good reason to worry.

The first scouts of the Soviet Army come riding into camp on motorcycles. The next few hours are joyous pandemonium as friendly Russian shock troops stream through our gates, bringing us meat, fresh vegetables, cheese and liquor they "liberated" from German farmhouses and cellars. We Kriegies eagerly stuff ourselves with food and swig down potent bottles of aquavit, promptly regretting it because our shrunken stomachs can't handle anything resembling a decent meal, much less high-test alcohol.

Following the shock troops come horse-drawn supply wagons with

Soviet Mongolians at the reins. To panicky German civilians, they might just as well have been the Genghis Khan hordes that swarmed over Eastern Europe in the 1200's.

We knew the Russians were coming, but we are surprised that the troops arrive as soon as they do. They would first have had to cross the Oder River, a major natural obstacle that figured to be very heavily fortified. We'd seen a steady stream of German tanks and troops going past camp toward the Oder to be reinforcements for the riverbank's defenders during the past week. However, they were mostly members of the Volksturm, the so-called People's Army. These were too young or too old for the regular Army, and hardly comparable to those Nazi goose-stepping elite warriors who conquered all Europe for the Fuhrer.

Meeting the Russian Commander... I Help Translate

Our Senior American Officer sends for a German-speaking Russian prisoner and me to be translators for a meeting with the Russian commander, a Colonel. That crossing of the Oder River is very much on our own senior officer's mind. Turning to me, he tells me to ask his Russian counterpart how it was done. The Russian prisoner relays the question.

"We sent the first wave over, and of course they were all killed," says the Russian officer. "We sent the second wave over, and most of them were killed. Ah, but the third wave went right through."

Now the Russian has a question for us. "Your great leader (President Roosevelt) has died. Why aren't you wearing black armbands?"

"We are in mourning," said our Colonel, "but we have no armbands to wear." We made some as soon as we could out of cloth scraps and lampblack.

Our Colonel has another question. The Russian troops have been waving their guns at some of our men, insisting that we leave camp because they have set us free. Could their commander please tell his troops we are waiting to be evacuated by air? We have orders from SHAEF, the Senior Headquarters of the American Expeditionary Force in Paris, to stay put until they can set up an airlift to bring us out to France.

When I relay that one through the interpreter the Russian Colonel smiles. "I will give you weapons," he says. "If my men give you trouble, just shoot them."

Our SAO gives me a startled look. "Lieutenant, are you sure that's what he said? Just shoot them?"

"Yes sir, but I'll ask again."

I get the same reply, with the Russian translator vigorously nodding his head.

"That's what he said, sir," I tell him.

"Hmmm," says the SAO. A chilling thought.

Second Thoughts About Our Russki Rescuers

In fact our senior officers have been having sobering thoughts about being in Russian hands. Our liberators are genuinely friendly and helpful, that's clear enough. But, what if their superiors decide to hang on to us as bargaining chips in future talks with the western allies?

SHAEF commanders have the same concerns because problems between the Soviet high command and the western allies are already surfacing. Our authorities in Paris order an airlift to begin immediately. Eventually, those disagreements over postwar Germany would escalate to the Cold War.

Miguel's Story

Meanwhile hundreds of Kriegies who just can't stand the idea of waiting around for an airlift begin to slip away from camp through torn gaps in the barbed wire fences, despite Kriegie guards posted by Col. Zemke to keep them all safely together until we're airlifted out. Most of them will make it to American or British lines, but a few come to grief in the chaos of the war's end. Several Kriegies who commandeered a car got drunk and were killed when the car ran into a ditch. Another was found dead with his throat slit. One of the Kriegies who headed for the American lines was my roommate buddy, fighter pilot Miguel Encinias. When I caught up with him after the war he told me why he didn't wait for the airlift: "It was just a feeling," he said. "I figured we're free, so let's get the hell out of here."

Miguel and three pilot buddies first stocked up at the camp warehouse on Red Cross chocolate bars to eat on the road, and a carton of cigarettes apiece as gifts to ease their way past the Russians they expected to encounter. Then they headed for nearby Barth in hopes of "liberating" some crayons to decorate the backs of their jackets with American flags. That was so Russian troops wouldn't think they were

Germans and shoot them. They found some crayons in town, created their flags, and then started walking west toward the Allied lines. They soon came to a farmhouse where five Germen women rushed out to greet them, recognizing them as ex-prisoners from the camp nearby. The women were crying and managed to get the idea over that the Russians had raped them all. It was a distressing story Miguel and his companions would hear often in the next three days, but as he said, "what could four guys do about it?" There were no male Germans to be seen anywhere, except at one Russian checkpoint where an English-speaking German tried to pass himself off as an American from New Mexico. Miguel, who came from New Mexico, wasn't fooled, and neither were the Russians who led him away to some unknown fate.

Miguel and his buddies spent the night as guests at the farmhouse. Horse drawn wagons with Russian Mongol troops at the reins kept going by, filled with supplies and military support personnel. One Russian who saw Mike and his pals go into the farm house stopped by and gave Miguel a bag of sugar as a token of friendship. Next morning Miguel put that sugar to good use, making fudge for his buddies to eat on the road. Then they set out for the Allied lines again, passing one Russian checkpoint after another by yelling, "Tovarich!" (Comrade) and handing out packs of cigarettes to the smiling Russkis. Thanks to Russians who gave them a series of rides, they made it to the Canadian lines near Hamburg in three days. The Canadians welcomed them as the first ex-prisoners they'd seen, gave them showers and clean clothing, and made arrangements to fly them to a British air base north of London. Examined and pronounced okay at a hospital there, they were put on a train to London and housed for the next three weeks at a Duke's townhouse while trying to find a ride back to the USA. "There were a million of us Americans in Britain waiting to go home," said Miguel. But finally one of his buddies met an American liberty ship's captain in a bar who promised he'd take them to New York City if they'd show up in a week at the docks in Liverpool where he was anchored. "Sure enough he did," said Miguel, "Each of us had a little stateroom." After five days of smooth sailing, they were approaching New York. "Hey, look!" said one of Miguel's buddies. "There's the Statue of Liberty!" They began cheering and clapping each other on the back, elated to be back at last in the good old USA.

When Miguel found his way to his parent's home in New Mexico, his mom and dad were overjoyed. "I hadn't known that they had agonized for eight months before they heard from a ham radio operator that I was in prison camp," he said. "They didn't know all that time whether I was dead or alive." But unlike most of us ex-POW's who'd had our fill of war, Miguel wanted to get right back into a fighter plane and help finish the war against Japan! Why? "I wanted to be an ace," he said. "I'd shot down two bombers and a fighter, and needed two more victories to make it. Several of my friends were aces, and that's what I wanted to be more than anything else." After several weeks in rehab to regain some strength and get used to eating real meals again, he reported for active duty—but before he could go overseas again, the war ended with the atomic bomb dropped on Hiroshima. Miguel went on to a distinguished career in the Air Force, flying combat in both Korea and Viet Nam, and teaching pilots for our allies before retiring as a Lieutenant Colonel.

CHAPTER TWENTY-FOUR
AIRLIFT TO FREEDOM

Meanwhile, back at Stalag Luft I, a stream of American B-17 bombers coming to rescue us appears over our camp within 48 hours on May 12th—my 22nd birthday. What a present! Their mission is to evacuate every man in camp with all possible haste. My turn comes on the second day as we stand in jubilant lines, waiting to hop aboard. Every B-17 taking off is jammed full of joyous Kriegies on this dreamed-of day. As I scramble aboard, I find a place to stand on the bomb bay catwalk like a subway straphanger, shoulder to shoulder with other ex-prisoners, all the way to Paris. It is an immensely exhilarating feeling to be airborne and free at last, after fourteen often-despairing months behind barbed wire. Army trucks, waiting as we land at Orly Field, take us to a staging area called Camp Lucky Strike on the mud flats outside the port of Le Havre. (Lucky Strike? It was the practice, quaint though it sounds today, to name our temporary camps in France after American cigarettes.) Lucky Strike is where we'll stay, in tents under field conditions, until transport ships are available to take us home at last to the States. We are elated to learn we have a travel priority to be shipped home, right after the wounded.

Real Food!

Lining up at a huge mess tent with our cafeteria-style trays, we are served breakfast—the first decent meal for any of us since being shot down. Like a beggar at a banquet, I load up my tray with generous helpings of scrambled eggs, steaming oatmeal and several slices of—look at that!—white bread. Real, genuine, sure enough, white bread, fragrant as a bakery, with no sawdust. But I just can't eat that much at one time. My stomach has shrunk. So after stuffing myself with those blissful eggs for breakfast, I manage to re-stuff with the oatmeal for lunch, saving that bread slathered with butter for dinner. The bread is like cake, absolutely delicious.

There are hundreds of us scruffy ex-POW's at a briefing after breakfast. Camp administrators tell us we'll stay here until we sail for home on the first available transport. How soon will that be? They don't know. Probably not for a month or more. Meanwhile we can get passes to see the outside world, right? No. No?? As we all groan in dismay, camp officers say they are not set up to do this, and besides, nearby Le Havre is still considered chaotic and dangerous. They want us on standby, ready to go whenever a transport becomes available. This makes sense to them, but not to young men who've just spent a year or more behind barbed wire, totally deprived and isolated from all normal human existence. I leave that meeting almost sick with frustration to think we may be penned up again for another month or more. We'll still be prisoners, only this time the guards will be our own countrymen. Don't they have a clue as to what it was like to be shut away for so long in enemy hands? Don't they understand how much we long for the simple privilege of walking down a street among free people? As I sit in a tent on my Army cot, awash in self-pity, I suddenly realize why this is hitting me so hard. I've reached my limit. I just can't stand being penned up any longer by anybody, anywhere, for any reason, not even by fellow Americans who wish us well and want to send us home as soon as they can.

A Hare-Brained Idea

I share my bitter, aching disappointment with a tent mate who sympathizes and says he feels the same way I do. "This is no way to treat guys who've been locked up and half-starved," says Lt. Patrick Donnelly, a husky blond bombardier and former bus driver from Seattle. Donnelly tells me he's been talking to some of our fellow Kriegies here who walked out of Germany into Allied hands.

"They got to Paris and were told to report to headquarters at the Hotel Crillon. Guess what happened next?"

"Surprise me."

"They were given new uniforms and some back pay, and got to spend a day sightseeing in Paris before being bussed here."

"Wow!" I say. "Too bad we couldn't do that."

"Maybe we could," says he.

"Could what?"

"Go to Paris."

"Go to Paris? What are you talking about?"

Donnelly is getting excited.

"There's a plane that flies in and out of here from Paris every day. Camp officers use it."

I'd seen the plane landing on the camp's temporary steel mesh runway, but I didn't see Donnelly's point yet.

"So?"

"So if we could get aboard somehow and land in Paris, we could do the same thing as the other guys—turn ourselves in at the hotel like we just walked out of Germany, get some new uniforms and cash, and go out on the town."

I have to laugh.

"Donnelly, you're really 'round the bend.'" (That's how the Brits in our camp had described guys who just couldn't handle being prisoners).

"You are totally bananas. You're stir-crazy."

"The hell I am," he says. "There's so much going on around here, guys coming and going, nobody knowing what the other guy's doing—I think we could get away with it."

Donnelly is no dummy, and he's right about all the confusion at our rapidly growing camp. But I still think his notion of making our escape in the camp's own plane is a wacky, totally off-the-wall idea.

"You're talking trouble," I say. "As officers we're supposed to be gentlemen, not go AWOL!"

"Aw, c'mon, Parker. The war in Europe is over."

"Yeah, but—"

"But what? We're not on duty here. We're just sitting around in tents, waiting to be shipped out like so many gunny sacks dumped on a dock. Who's gonna give a damn as long as we come back in time to go home?"

141

It's starting to make sense, but it's still a wild and crazy idea. "Okay," I say, "but how could a couple of Kriegies like us get aboard a plane without being thrown off again? And what about roll call every morning?"

"Roll call's easy," says Donnelly. "We get a couple of guys in our tent to say 'Yo!' every morning when our names are called."

"Yeah, that'd probably work—but what about the plane? How in hell could we get away with it?"

The big question didn't faze him in the least. "Well, you're a navigator and I'm a bombardier. If anyone aboard asks questions, we tell 'em we have permission from headquarters for you to give me a navigation lesson."

I can't believe I'm hearing this. "Donnelly, that's ridiculous. Anybody who'd believe a cockamamie story like that is an idiot!"

"Maybe so, but what have we got to lose?"

He had me there.

CHAPTER TWENTY-FIVE

THE PARIS CAPER

Donnelly and I hang around the airstrip for a few days, quietly casing the airport's activities so we can plan our Paris caper. We soon discover that a C-47 flies in most afternoons with an officer or two involved with camp administration. By asking pilots a few discreet questions, we learn these flights all return to Paris. What could be better? On the other hand I am becoming a world-class worrywart about this bizarre scheme of ours. Either it's a terrific idea—great therapy for a couple of guys who've been shut-ins too long - or a disaster in the making. We'll soon know. We go over our final "break-out" plan, rehearsing as if we are commandos planning a drop in enemy territory. We intend to board a Paris-bound transport plane at the last possible moment, making it more difficult for anyone to stop us before takeoff. From what we see happening, it looks as if we really do have a good chance to pull this off. Paris in the spring, tra-la, tra-la! We say farewell the following summer morning to our tent mates who promise to answer roll calls for us, and set out for the landing strip.

While we're staking out the plane parked on the runway, the pilot shows up and starts the engines. We wait with mounting anxiety for fifteen minutes more until an Air Force Major from headquarters finally hurries out with his briefcase to board the plane. It's now or never. "Let's go!" says Donnelly, and we sprint to the aircraft. The Major seems quite surprised to see us come aboard and quietly sit down as if this were normal routine. There's obviously nothing routine about a ragtag pair of Kriegies boarding his flight to Paris. Fixing his gaze on me, he says, "What are you men doing on this plane?"

My mind goes blank. Tongue-tied, I turn to Donnelly. He takes over like the con man he truly could be, launching into a deliberately long-winded spiel to eat up time. I don't remember his exact words, but it went something like this:

"Well, sir, Lieutenant Parker here is a navigator, one of our best, sir. And I'm a bombardier with ambitions to be a navigator myself some day. I figure navigators will be in great demand after the war, but there probably won't be much call for bombardiers."

The Major doesn't look as if he's buying a word of this, but Donnelly keeps going with a spiel like a carnival barker:

"We're here at Camp Lucky Strike on temporary duty, you might say, sir, so I asked the Lieutenant to give me a navigation lesson. He was kind enough to agree, so that's why we're here, sir." The Major scowls at this preposterous story, as indeed he should, and sternly demands to know who authorized our flight. "Headquarters, sir," says Donnelly. Meanwhile I'm smiling and nodding despite feeling like an escaping convict caught in the searchlights. By now the pilot is revving the engines, ready for take-off. The Major, distracted by the engine roar, looks up the aisle toward the cockpit as if thinking of stopping the flight, but it's too late. The pilot releases the brakes and the plane gathers speed down the runway. The Major grumbles something to himself but says nothing further. We're on our way to Paris!

Fortunately for Donnelly and me, the Major spends the flight going through papers in his briefcase. Evidently he has no further interest in us. We aren't his problem, and he's not ours. It's a beautiful afternoon toward the end of May, with fluffy clouds floating by the windows as we approach Paris. We can see the Eiffel Tower as the plane turns and sets down on the runway. Donnelly and I are grinning like mischievous little kids and give each other exuberant thumbs-up. A French phrase comes to mind that I learned from a Louisiana Cajun cadet: "Laissez les bon temps roulez"—Let the good times roll! As the plane taxies to a stop, the Major gives us one more skeptical glance but says nothing. Then the door swings open and he goes down the steps and out of our lives.

We get off moments later, anxious to avoid the pilot who probably isn't even aware he brought two stowaways along. We try to hitch a ride into town with a B-17 pilot who has just landed. Smooth-as-butter Donnelly tells him we're ex-POW's on our way to report in at the world-famous Hotel Crillon. The pilot is happy to drive us there. This hotel was and still is one of the finest in the world, which is undoubtedly why American military leaders chose it for a headquarters. Its Presidential Apartment has been favored in recent years by such cash-laden celebrities as Madonna and film star/Governor Arnold Schwarzenegger. The price is rumored so exorbitant that it's only revealed after you've confirmed your reservation. Guests wealthy enough to afford a suite can sit on their big fat terraces and look down the Champs Elysees to the Arc de Triomphe.

A Taste Of The High Life

The incredibly deluxe Crillon, tastefully renovated in the Louis XV style, is right next door to the spot where rebellious peasants once chopped off the heads of aristocrats. I guess this proves that while the poor are always with us, the rich shall rise again. Into all this magnificence come Donnelly and I, the ultimate contrast in our sloppy fatigues to the glittering jet set guests. The desk clerk smiles and directs us upstairs where we are welcomed, signed in, outfitted in smart new uniforms, issued mess passes for dinner at this very hotel, *and* given cash from our back pay. "Oh, and take these, too," says a Sergeant who brings us each a huge handful of condoms wrapped in gold foil. "There's a dance downstairs tonight for military personnel. You might get lucky." Donnelly and I stuff the golden gifts into our pockets and hurry back downstairs for a feast in the restaurant.

As we walk through the lobby in our fresh military regalia, including those silver wings that are said to melt girls' hearts, two luscious looking U.S Army nurses approached us. Va-va-va-voom!

"Do you gentlemen have mess passes?" the blonde one asks. For once I speak up before Donnelly can open his mouth. "We sure do."

"We don't have passes ourselves," says the blonde, "but you're allowed to have guests." Obviously these two are chowhounds who've been dining out on Kriegies. I can only admire their enterprise.

"Hey, please join us," said Donnelly. I could swear he was licking his lips. As I hastily yank the mess pass out of my pants pocket to show the ladies, a cascade of those gold-foiled gizmos spills out and scatters across the floor. Sacre bleu! How embarrassing! I pounce on them with both hands to stuff them back in my pants, faster than a pickpocket. As

I straighten up, Donnelly and both nurses are looking up at the hand-painted ceiling as if nothing has happened. Donnelly finally manages to say, "Shall we go to the dining room?" Both nurses nod. Hunger does that to people.

As I look back half-a-century to that awkward scene, I'm just glad we were available to feed those poor starving girls. They shovel in the calories as if they've been dieting for weeks. Without so much as a thank you or an au revoir, they pat their lips with their napkins, say the briefest of goodbyes, and leave us sitting there like a pair of punched meal tickets. I could only conclude that these angels of mercy had patients to look after, and thus had to deny themselves the pleasure of our company for the rest of the evening. Oh, well…I wouldn't want to go dancing with the likes of us either. Not after seeing that golden surprise on the lobby floor.

Swinging At the Ball

We head for the ballroom where a band is playing American swing tunes for a capacity crowd of jitterbugging soldiers, airmen and local femmes. Donnelly seeks out a petite brunette on the sidelines, I find a rather regal looking brunette, and in moments Donnelly and I are on the dance floor with live, female, human beings. My date radiates a heady French perfume that blends with the warm and intimate essence of a dancing woman. I am beginning to think I have indeed gotten "lucky," as the Sergeant put it. She murmurs a few caressing syllables in my ear that sound ever so romantic, but seeing my blank look, she asks, "Sprechen Sie Deutsch?" I eagerly confess that I understand some German, so we spend the rest of the evening dancing while I struggle to make conversation. After the ball is over, I offer to escort her home in a cab.

"No thank you," she says in delightfully accented English, "But I've had a lovely evening." I'm bewildered by her sudden switch in languages.

"If you understand English," I say, "How come we've been talking German all night?" She smiles.

"I haven't had a chance to speak it since the Germans were driven out of Paris."

Of all the girls at that dance, I had to pick a linguist who prefers to go home by herself.

Next morning Donnelly and I check out early. We have no intention of joining other Kriegies on that bus we're supposed to catch going to Camp Lucky Strike. Been there. Done that. No way! Not while we are clad in smart new uniforms with wads of francs in our pockets, intent on having a high time in gay Paree.

The first thing we need to do is find another place to stay. We begin checking out various lesser hotels along the boulevards, with no luck whatever. It seems that SHAEF had requisitioned all these hostelries for its own personnel who've been running the war in Europe. Finally we find a small hotel that actually welcomes us. An elfin creature, slim as a model and clad in naught but a chemise opens the door and beckons for us to come in. Donnelly and I exchange glances. What kind of a hotel is this?

The mystery is solved in moments when an older Mademoiselle appears and explains in English that this is a place where gentlemen come to seek the company of young ladies—a house of joy, as they say in France. But there are also rooms for rent, she says. Would we want rooms? We would. The next several days are a merry blur of sightseeing, stuffing ourselves at restaurants and reveling in general, all of it lasting until our bankrolls dwindle to small change. Ah, what a wondrous way to celebrate our re-entry into the world of free beings!

Breaking Back Into Camp

But now reality is tapping us on the shoulder. It's time to get back to Camp Lucky Strike, lest we miss the big boat ride back to the good old USA. We spend our last few francs on a cab ride to Orly Field. Then we start checking out all the American warplanes touching down there, hoping to hitch a ride.

We soon locate the friendly pilot of a B-17 who thinks he can assist us. He and his navigator fish out an aerial map of Western France. The pilot frowns as he studies it. "I don't see that camp listed anywhere near Le Havre."

"I'm not surprised," I say. "It's a temporary camp with a metal mesh landing strip."

"What makes you think we can land a B-17 there anyhow?" he asks. Donnelly jumps in to close the sale. "C-47's land there every day." he says.

"Oh," says the pilot. "I'd like to help you guys, but I can't unless you can find that camp for me."

"I can do that," I say. I remember what the terrain looks like from the air.

The pilot purses his lips and stares off into space, pondering.

"Tell you what, gentlemen," he says. "We're heading back to London.

If you can find that landing strip, I'll set you down there. If you can't, you're going to London with us. Deal?"

"Deal." say I.

We shake hands, and soon we are taking off for what we hope will be Camp Lucky Strike. As we near the coast by Le Havre, I spot the camp right where I thought it would be. "If you don't mind," I say to the pilot, "it would help if you'd make a steep approach and touch down just long enough to let us out. Otherwise all the ex-prisoners will crowd around the plane to see who's aboard, and you might get stuck there a while." I'm engaging in a bit of gamesmanship here. The real reason I'm suggesting a steep approach and swift takeoff is that we hope to slip away before the brass comes out and sees us.

"Good idea," says the pilot.

True to his word, he sets the bomber down on the temporary runway and hits the brakes. The moment we jump out onto the runway, he slams the throttles forward to roar back into the sky as camp staffers watch in some bewilderment, wondering what just happened. Meanwhile Donnelly and I melt into the gathering crowd of ex-Kriegies, and head back to our tent. Had the authorities noticed we'd been missing? No, our tent mates had covered for us at every roll call. Was there any news about a ship to take us home? Yes, a transport is due in port within a week or so, with room for us all. Ah, how sweet it is!

Homeward Bound!

After a week's rest in camp and more of that sensational, sawdust-free food the Army keeps heaping on our plates, we are trucked down to the dock at Le Havre. There lies an Army transport with its gangplank down, ready to take us aboard. Soon we'll be voyaging home to the USA, destination Newport News, Virginia. It's hard to believe that this ultimate in Kriegie fantasies is really happening.

We all board the transport during the first week in June. The weather is so warm that it's stifling in our hammocks below decks, so we decide to sleep on the main deck. By day we laze in the sun and play bridge for money. Since I'd had such a good bridge teacher in Four Engine Jones, I come away with a fistful of real American dollars. After several pleasant days of sailing in calm seas, the cry goes up, "Land ho!" We rush to the railings to see the USA again at long, long last. We shout and wave and dance around and jump up and down and hug each other, teary with joy. *We made it! We're back! We're home!!!* That USA coastline looming before us is the vision that has sustained us during all those months of hunger and privation, never knowing whether we'd see our loved ones again. It's the happiest day of our lives, now and forever more, and I for one will never forget it, not ever.

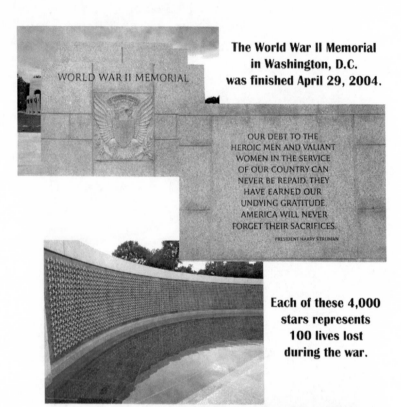

WORLD WAR II MEMORIAL

The World War II Memorial
in Washington, D.C.
was finished April 29, 2004.

OUR DEBT TO THE
HEROIC MEN AND VALIANT
WOMEN IN THE SERVICE
OF OUR COUNTRY CAN
NEVER BE REPAID. THEY
HAVE EARNED OUR
UNDYING GRATITUDE.
AMERICA WILL NEVER
FORGET THEIR SACRIFICES.
PRESIDENT HARRY S TRUMAN

Each of these 4,000
stars represents
100 lives lost
during the war.

THE REST OF THE STORY

There's a saying, "If you want to make God laugh, tell him your plans." As a boy during the Great Depression, when twelve million Americans were unemployed and my family was on relief, I spent hour after hour reading books in the local library, caught up in adventure stories like "Robinson Crusoe" and swashbuckling tales like "Captains Courageous" and "Treasure Island" that took me on adventures to faraway places. I began to think of becoming an author myself some day, or perhaps an English teacher, or even a professor. But, by the time I turned seventeen in May 1940, Nazi Germany had just overrun France with fast moving columns of tanks and blitzkrieg (lightning war) tactics. More than 300,000 British troops had to be rescued off the beaches of Dunkirk, abandoning all their guns and ammunition. A month later, I was giving a high school graduation speech about Hitler enslaving Europe and the threat of war coming to our own doorstep.

Then it was my turn to serve, in combat and prison camp, during almost four years in uniform. After qualifying for a discharge from the Air Corps with a fistful of points for time served, I felt much too impatient to spend four more years to become an academic. Instead, I gratefully went back to work for the Los Angeles Examiner, writing bylined features and eventually being promoted to the rewrite desk. Then an attractive offer from the L.A. Times came along, but after a pleasant year there I became convinced that there'd be a big future for writers in a brand new medium called television.

At first, there wasn't much to look at or write about on that small black and white screen. A popular TV show in Los Angeles, for example, was a guy on a bare stage playing the organ. But, people would stand shoulder to shoulder on the sidewalk outside store windows each night to watch this amazing new invention "showing" live programs. I applied for a public relations job at CBS-TV so I'd be on the inside to find out where I might fit. One client who liked my work was a big star of the Fifties and Sixties, emcee Art Linkletter. He hired me as head writer of his top-rated daytime show, "Art Linkletter's House Party." I stayed with this delightfully amiable, quick-witted and fun-loving performer for a dozen years until the show ended its run in the late Sixties. I then spent three years on staff writing comedy material for Bob Hope, and several more in charge of writers for Hanna-Barbera Studios for popular animated shows ranging from "Yogi Bear" to "Scooby Doo" and "The Smurfs." My last major assignment before retiring was supervising the writing for 64 half-hour shows for a children's educational program called "Zoobilee Zoo," created by Hallmark. It featured singers and dancers in animal costumes, and starred Ben Vereen, the Tony Award-winning Broadway song and dance man.

As retirees, my wife Ethel and I roamed the west in an RV, searching for a small town with a college and a variety of activities for seniors to enjoy. Our favorite turned out to be Durango, Colorado, in the foothills of the San Juan Mountains. Its offerings include Ft. Lewis College and its Community Concert Hall, the San Juan Symphony, the Durango Arts Center, and all kinds of other musical and artistic events. We also learned to ski, which was great fun. It took me three seasons to entice Ethel onto the slopes. Once she tried it, she loved it so much she didn't want to come down again! After two very satisfying decades of living in Durango, enjoying close friendships and happy to stay for the rest of our lives, doctors advised us that Ethel needed to return to sea level for her health. So, we packed up, returned to Southern California and resettled in Santa Monica to be close to three of our grown children who live nearby. We keenly miss the friends that we had to leave behind, but we've stayed in touch and visit back and forth whenever it works out. Meanwhile Ethel's feeling like her old self again and enjoying a full, active life – and so am I.

EPILOGUE

THOUGHTS ABOUT WAR

We must never forget the sacrifices of young Americans who went off to serve their country in wartime, and never came back. We must never forget their comrades who were maimed and crippled in both body and mind. In this book I wanted to be a faithful witness to the terror and mindless horror that war is, and to offer a testament against it. Some day leaders have to learn that war is no longer an option for human beings.

War gave me and millions of others a first-hand acquaintance with death. It taught us that life was finite and could end at any time. That no one in wartime could count on any kind of normal existence, the kind that comes with marriage, a family and a career. We had to survive first to have any kind of life at all. The reality that life could end at any moment dominated our whole existence. It was truly frightening to know comrades all around you were dying, their lives ending before they'd really begun. When would it be your turn? Or would you survive?

War made me thoughtful, reflective, serious about life, grateful every time I escaped death to live another day. In combat I learned that life was on the line with every flight and I felt trapped and powerless. How did I get to such a desperate point in my life? Was this it? Was it all to end so randomly? Why me? Was I someone trying to be my best, or just a naïve young fool, recklessly hurling himself in harm's way? Would I never have a wife, or children? Was there nothing to look forward to, ever again? I had no presentiments, one way or the other. I didn't expect to live or die. I just had to keep keeping on.

In prison I learned to adapt to what had to be, to live what there was of life within the strict boundaries of the reality of a prison run by the enemy. I made up my mind to survive, come what may. In aerial combat I was both terrified and numb with resignation to whatever might happen. In prison camp I did my best to enjoy my companions and hang on to our hopes for the future. But often, in the dark of the night, the sheer monotonous, unendingness of it all broke me down. I wondered how much more of this I could take.

The most important thing any human has is freedom. When it is taken away from you, you are not really you any more. You are in an emotional limbo, just waiting, waiting, waiting...and worst of all it is like an indeterminate sentence in any prison. You don't know when it will end, or whether you will survive to go home when it's over.

Many young people today, inheritors of liberty paid for with the blood of their grandfathers, wonder why these old veterans seldom if ever talk about their wartime experiences. It's because they remember. In the silence of the night come unbidden memories and dreadful dreams of comrades shrieking in agony and dying. It's almost impossible to talk about such memories without reliving them—and no survivor of combat wants to do that.

In war, as in life, you take what you get. If you come home, you try to put your life back together. Some men do this better than others, depending on what happened to them and whatever strength they can still call upon inside themselves. Other men have seen too much, suffered too much and mourned too much to be anything like their pre-war selves ever again. How could it be otherwise?

I have a confession to make, because I owe it to other veterans, past and present, to make it. I don't want anyone to think that you can go through this kind of trauma without it having a lasting effect on you. I came home after World War II with what is now known as PTSD—Post Traumatic Stress Disorder. I was a nervous wreck, prone to nightmares, drinking too much, smoking three packs a day and popping tranquilizer pills, but I had no idea I was suffering from a medical disorder. PTSD wasn't officially recognized as such until 1980, 35 years after WWII. Even then I didn't find out I had it until I started research on this book in 2000. Memories came flooding back in full force as if I'd opened a Pandora's Box, setting loose all those jittery, scary, fearful emotions I'd slammed the lid on after the war. I began debating whether I might be better off dropping the whole idea of writing a wartime memoir —but finally decided I had to hang in there and do it. Fortunately I talked to other combat vets, members of the Eighth Air Force Historical Society in Albuquerque, who told me I could get counseling and help at the Veterans Administration Hospital there. That is how, more than half a century after WWII, I got the expert counseling and guidance I needed. I believe to this day that those group therapy sessions with other vets as well as private counseling saved my marriage. They gave both my beloved wife and me an understanding of what we were really dealing with, and renewed our faith in staying together for the past 45 years.

I'd like to say why I think understanding and coping with PTSD is important enough to me that I felt compelled to add it to the end of my book. This disorder can cause a great deal of unintended harm. It often

154

goes unrecognized for what it is and can last for years and years, as I have reason to know. PTSD not only hurt my marriage, but also had an effect on all of my relationships—including those with our children. The sooner that PTSD is recognized and treated the better off everyone will be. There is a better life beyond PTSD. I feel that I've had my life handed back to me, and that's a very good thing.

As Gen. William Tecumseh Sherman famously said during the Civil War, "War is hell." And he said it generations before the atomic hells of Hiroshima and Nagasaki. What would Sherman have said if he knew that mighty, previously unknown weapons—just two atomic bombs —could kill over 100,000 human beings and injure nearly 100,000 more, all within a mile and a half of their detonations? We can only hope that our leaders and others around the world will work together with renewed urgency to avoid any future atomic war by creating lasting peace among all nations.

FOOTNOTES

Foreword:
[1]Excerpt from "Bombers of WWII" by Jeffrey L. Ethell, Lowe & B. Hould Publishers.

[2] Air University Review, January-February 1971.

[3] British writer Ian Hawkins.

Chapter 10:
[4] USAF medical research program at High Wycombe, Buckinghamshire, UK.

Chapter 18:
[5] "FighterPilot, Alelutians to Normandy to Stalag Luft I, Mozart Kaufman.

Chapter 20:
[6] "Zemke's Stalag," Smithsonian Institution Press, as told to Roger A. Freeman.

[7] "Zemke's Stalag," Smithsonian Institution Press, by Zemke as told to Roger A. Freeman.

PHOTO CREDITS

The National Archives
The National Archives of the United Kingdom
www.merkki.com (photos of the POW-WOWs)
USAF Major General Don Ross
George Luke & Family (photos of Stalag Luft 1)
Colonel Jean R. Byerly, Lynda Byerly Stuges and
Captain Robert B. Byerly
Colonel Henry "Russ" Spicer & Family
World War II Memorial photos provided by Mark C. Bonn

CPSIA information can be obtained
at www.ICGtesting.com
Printed in the USA
LVOW10s2332230817
546171LV00001B/267/P